THE
ZONE
OF
HOLINESS

THE
ZONE
OF
HOLINESS

New Possiblities for Materializing
Your Heart's Desire

LINDA NORWOOD

SUNSTONE
PRESS

SANTA FE

Sunstone books may be purchased for educational, business, or sales promotional use.
For information please write: Special Markets Department, Sunstone Press,
P.O. Box 2321, Santa Fe, New Mexico 87504-2321.

Book and Cover design › Vicki Ahl
Body typeface › Adobe Jenson Pro
Printed on acid-free paper
∞
eBook 978-1-61139-262-3

Library of Congress Cataloging-in-Publication Data

Norwood, Linda, 1943-
  The zone of holiness : new possibilities for materializing your heart's desire / by Linda
Norwood.
      pages cm
  Includes bibliographical references.
  ISBN 978-0-86534-414-3 (softcover : alk. paper)
  1. Spiritual life. 2. Holiness. I. Title.
  BL624.N677 2014
  204'.4--dc23

                              2014006624

WWW.SUNSTONEPRESS.COM
SUNSTONE PRESS / POST OFFICE BOX 2321 / SANTA FE, NM 87504-2321 /USA
(505) 988-4418 / ORDERS ONLY (800) 243-5644 / FAX (505) 988-1025

To Andrea, Bach and Nicholas
For keeping Mom connected to Earth

Contents

Preface / 9
Acknowledgments / 14
Note to Readers / 15
Prologue / 17

1 Finding the Holy Zone in Everyday Life / 25
2 My Story / 38
3 The Power of Protocol / 53
4 The Do(s) of Life / 69

    A. The Basics / 69

    B. Lagniappe / 96

5 The Seven Doors to Energy Freedom / 107

    The Yellow Door / 109

    The Green Door / 111

    The Blue Door / 119

    The Orange Door / 121

    The Red Door / 124

    The Purple Door / 127

    The White Door / 131

6 The Don'ts of Life / 134
7 Who Controls What / 146
8 Ten Finger Friends in Meditation / 151
9 What to Do When You Feel Bad and Sad / 163
10 The Voice: A Catalystic Frontier / 169
11 Jesus Christ and Cell Memory / 181
12 Sex in the Holy Zone / 197

Epilogue / 202
Resources and Bibliography / 205

Preface

Moving with Universal laws to the eternal music of creation and resting in the ebb and flow, I am free to be all I am. Some feelings, revelations, and thoughts can be best expressed with poetry. When symbolism conveys the idea, the communication is efficient beyond reason. Within the scope of poetry is the mystery and history of words that have power beyond our human means and intentions. This is why they are best used with great respect. Words can be instruments of holiness or instruments of profanity. Where logic is insufficient, poetry can take over and create a bridge between mind and soul. May it be so here.

"Who are you and what do you want!!" I shouted back through the locked door—awakened by the sound of a motor vehicle stopped just outside my tiny room next to the real tack room, in the horse quarters. Someone was shaking the door lock trying to enter. "What? It must be midnight!" I thought. A woman's voice—short with frustration shouted from outside the closed door: "Oh someone's already in it!"

When I heard the voice I felt safe enough to open the door, held to by a chain lock, just wide enough to see a young woman standing on the narrow covered porch, spotlighted as if on stage, by the blast of headlights from a small silver car. Golden lengths of hair casually framed her pleasantly lined face, focused by life, the requirements of the moment and revealed by the faint but vigilant porch light.

"Yes, this is my room!" I confirmed, realizing that the situation was harmless. This woman was a fellow student arriving for Jinshindo® Acupressure class from somewhere, in the middle of the night, looking for the place she was assigned to for the duration. She was brave to come down that rugged, winding drive so late at night. My third, unspoken question was "What are you going to do?" So many important things come in threes

"There is a room next to this one, but no lights" I informed her.

"It's locked!" she lamented. "On no—it's open!—I can see a bed, I think, on the floor."

"Here—you can use this flashlight. It's extra." I had provisions a-plenty in my room.

"Oh, thank you—I'll sleep here." The blonde was fixing to be settled. I could close the door and go back to bed. She had reserved the tack room with saddles and harnesses on the walls. I chose the room next to it with electricity and a small window. The Ranch director must have been exasperated with my emails with so many questions, insisting to know—among other things—the window size and whether it could be opened. Air and water quality are huge with me. I had to know if I could function in California for the ten-day stretch to learn the next level of Acupressure. The open spaces of this Ranch and the dry, cool air of April seemed to be free of noticeable pollution. Water—oh yes—right next to the room, outside. The horses and I had water. I learned later how really good it was. There was a wide metal sink with a facet where I could get drinking water and brush my teeth. I was almost home. I loved it. My neighbor was on her own. I would help her if I could, but she seemed quite self-sufficient.

I left my comforts in Louisiana, and drove over two thousand miles for this venue and opportunity. All I had to do was take care of myself and learn. Before I loaded the truck and left for California, so many incidents and situations arose to stop me, but the Spirit said "go follow" and I did. What an adventure for me at sixty-four—a regrouping, married, female, artist, mother, lawyer and user of Acupressure with one basic class under my belt. I wanted some tools to heal with and help others. Experiencing energy work brought on daily revelations of how the future of physical body care would look for mankind. I believed and still believe that it must upgrade and become more preventative—something a person can mostly do for himself.

Who are you? What do you want? What are you going to do?
I pondered and drove.

Life gets to be quite basic at times, as it was that night on the edge of the horse pasture in California. Those are the times when the questions we need answered are easy and so are the answers. Then there are other times—subtle crossroads for choice—with the same questions. These times are probably the most important. They happen all through the day and sometimes in the night. These choices define us and determine what happens in our life story. These subtle crossroads may be the very ones that the Adversary Spirit "notices." The daily choices may seem small to us and insignificant. Being off guard, we are easily led astray unless we are aware of the "Blessings Game" and the two Voices that contend for our time, energy, and everything we are.

The adversary is a powerful, contrary spirit to the other Spirit—of God, our Advocate. He or "it" is able to detect our spiritual energy frequency. This adversary spirit is ready to deceive us with great cunning. I suspect the adversary cannot read our thoughts or our written words, yet picks us up on some specific frequency. Someday, this theory will be as obvious as the sun and moon. For now, it is a revelation that I cannot prove or withhold from you. Keeping us outside the Zone of Holiness is the driving purpose of the evil one. The zone of profanity is easily attractive until our eyes become open to the truth.

This writing exposes the game plan of the adversary and the rules of the Advocate that protect us. When you understand how the author of lies works, you have the power to avoid the zone where he dwells—the zone of profanity. The rewards are tremendous when we make our best choices. You can learn how to choose well to the level of an automatic skill. You can draw unto your self and your loved ones gifts and blessings beyond your dreams. You can be an instrument that the Universe uses to bless—in unplanned, surprising, and healing ways. Those you teach then teach others. The beginning is right where you are now.

Some unusual spiritual theories are explored here. This is a primer in everyday, practical, powerful Life Protocol. You can consciously reject the spiritual correlations and concepts here, yet receive many of the benefits if you understand and apply the daily principles offered. Don't let reason stand in the way of truth. Logic is a limited tool given to us by the Creator to get us from point A to point B routine. Pure logic cannot tell me who I am or what I want. Spiritual truth is the inspiration for mankind's progress. Science merely confirms and helps it materialize. At the same time, technology in the hands of evil threatens the existence of mankind today. This book addresses the problem and offers a solution.

I discover *who I am* when I make choices outside of habit, with integrity. I only know specifically *what I want* when I get it. To know *what to do*, I have learned some Universal rules and try to follow them every day. These simple life rules are shown here. My quest is to be at the right place, at the right time, with the right people, doing the right thing for the right reason. I cannot succeed in this quest by planning and organized effort. It is beyond my means but not beyond my ability to attain.

The way God works with us, is a process called the "Blessings Game." The tension in the game is between God and the powers of evil. It is discussed here and shown to be the arena of spiritual activity that immediately affects our physical life. It is about seeing through lies. If you can do that, you blow Satan's cover. If you blow his cover and move even a bit into the Zone of Holiness, you win.

May you find your way into the Zone of Holiness, as far beyond the curse of evil as possible in this world—if you're not there already there. May you see how the "Blessings Game" and how you play it makes the difference—in living with holiness or living with profanity. The rules of the game are in the chapters following. Everyone plays—with or without awareness of the rules and stakes.

Acknowledgments

For reading, for sharing their thoughts and responses, for encouragement and advice, I want to thank the following fellow adventurers: Jim Norwood, Richard Bradley, Bach Norwood, Donna Dunlop, Sherry Mills Sneller, and Nicole LeBlanc Arnold.

For helping me daily to interface with the world of technology, I especially thank Joshua Pate and Andrea Norwood Pate.

For encouraging me to keep going with this book when I felt like keeping it all to myself, I thank Nicholas Norwood.

Note to Readers

Every kind of care has been taken to insure this book is true to the revelations given me by the Spirit. Even when a spiritual concept awaits scientific notice in the ways of mankind, I have not withheld it from you.

The responsibility for your well-being and evolvement is yours alone. I offer ideas and personal experience here for you to use however the Advocate Spirit directs. The content of this book is not intended as a substitute for medical advice or care, but as a complement. My intent is to give you a safe and powerful way to avoid the pitfalls of modern life and have found the concepts here in *The Zone of Holiness* to be a vital link to my own and mankind's birthright of health.

Wherever you are and whatever your age, may you find, as you read, the inspiration to materialize the love you are, with a new awareness and confidence. It is never too soon to begin following your dreams and never too late to have some.

—Linda Norwood

Prologue

There are two main spiritual zones—holiness and profanity. Holiness will be reckoned with here. Delving into the zone of profanity would give it energy. Profanity is what holiness is not. There is no neutral zone although holy energy vibrations differ in intensity and power, as do the energy vibrations of the profane. These zones of holiness and profanity are materialized in the world. They are materialized in our bodies. I offer you here the revelations that have come to me from searching, praying, watching, listening and experimenting. The more I live beyond my natural means, by following the Spirit's direction, the better my life. This writing is good to the extent it is beyond my natural means. In this book I explore the practical side of following the Spirit and share with you the logic I call "spiritual science." I am particularly interested in the type of inspiration that is earthly good, yet I am dependent on something that is beyond this earth—something I lean upon for help. As the blossom of the yellow *Dusty Miller* leans to the sun, I lean to that some One—God—mankind's immediate sustainer and hope for the future. When we lean on other persons, we take the risk that they will unexpectedly move and leave us sprawling.

I want more goodness in my days and nights than I can expect from other human beings and more than I can expect from myself. Instead of being frustrated or disappointed, I have learned to depend on God to meet my needs. This is the essence of what I call the Blessings Game. I have enjoyed playing games to win since I was a child. I loved to play checkers and Monopoly until I became aware of the truth that it meant nothing if I won or if I lost. If I won, someone else lost and felt bad. If I lost, someone else won and I felt bad. This kind of game playing never contributed much to the emotional quality of our family/friendship gatherings. As time passed, these games became boring. They were much ado about nothing. I wanted much more from the use of my time and energy. Only later in my life did I begin to understand the real life game I write about here. Certainly, the blessings God gives are often through another person, or even through myself. Nevertheless, to allow the Almighty One to provide in the area of our greatest need, is where the real joy and peace and power in life resides. To know how far to go to help oneself and when to stop and wait on the Lord, is the skill that makes all the difference in our quality of life. The person highly skilled in this area draws the energy of blessings automatically by being in the position and condition to receive them. Knowing how to apply the rules of the Blessings Game affects our quality of life in the areas that mean the most to us. In this area we do not compare ourselves to or with other persons. It is entirely personal and individual. In the Blessings Game we learn who we are, what we really want, and how to get it.

The focus of *dependence* is what makes the initial difference as we begin to experience the effect of our choices in the Blessings Game. After a person reaches a place of accountability (awareness/responsibility) in life, it is actually profane to depend on another person or even on self for the important things in life: venue for home and work, health, love, peace and joy, and material provisions. This concept is contrary to the way of the world we live in. We may find a good place to work and live, take reasonable care of ourselves, love, have some peace and joy and make money without *conscious dependence* or focus on God, yet we short circuit the power in these vital areas when we do our living without being aware of this divine relationship—the good in our lives is not the best it could be. We can *say* we depend on God, yet live as though it all depends on us or on someone else in our lives and miss divine appointments, pivotal events happening, and special people appearing in our lives. The acknowledged, authentic and conscious dependence on God for the blessings we desire in life, at the crux of choice, is practical holiness.

In everyday choices and actions, we can claim the power of dependence and receive divine blessings. This skill takes awareness, faith and patience. Once learned, it is valuable beyond imagination or measure. The Zone of Holiness becomes familiar. When choices are made that takes us into profanity and out of holiness, we see the results and take note. Strength develops within our life environment of people and things and nature. We have much then to share and teach. This result of learning the Blessings Game and living in the Zone of Holiness is richness and "winning" that matters. You may experience physical abundance beyond your basic need, or for some mysterious reason, your success may be immaterial, as you make holy choices. The rules of the Game I have found are here to inspire your own experience of discovery.

The name of this book and the driving themes appeared consciously after it was ninety percent finished. When I discovered the name of this book, then all its parts began to fit together into an organic whole. *The Zone of Holiness* was the name of something I had been looking for all my life. I was destined to discover the Zone of Holiness concept and the Blessings Game dynamics at the time in my life that I could write with enough past experience to understand them. The spiritual battle here on earth that underlies all other battles is self-blessing versus divine blessing. It is the contest between holiness and profanity. As we take small steps of faith and refuse to self-bless, awaiting the divine response, the adventure begins. As we stay true to our vision of holiness and waiting on the Lord, the result is something we can build upon forever. It is our solid foundation. At this point we begin to build spiritual strength and bank spiritual resources.

In the pages that follow, there is a daily plan of practical structure for the days and nights to use and observe—a Protocol of Life. With this Protocol as a guide for creating your own Protocol of Life, you have a vehicle to use for entering into the Zone of Holiness, level by level, at your own perfect rate of speed, blessing by blessing. Once the mindset of holiness versus profanity begins to take root, everything in your life is affected and improved—automatically. Your nervous system organizes itself to accomplish holy works without your conscious planning or effort. It becomes your good friend rather than something of an irritation as it was when you resisted holiness. We are designed to love and move towards the Zone of Holiness, yet the influences of the evil one can trick us into making profane choices as we are tempted to do what is sensually attractive, convenient and easy. Embrace the initial feelings of unsettlement as you set your intentions towards holiness and move to a new level of the spirit. New plants disturb the soil as they emerge from seed.

***

I have always had a sensitive nervous system and have noticed that I am relaxed and comfortable with some people, and with some places and situations. With others, I am nervous to the point of being almost frantic to get away. I move on away now without feeling guilty. I know it is the right thing to do. This ultra sensitivity I have to people, places and situations, taste, smell, touch and sound has been interpreted to me by one of my teachers in energy work, as the awareness of "spiritual warfare." It does often feel like a *battle* to defend myself against the deception and devices of the profane and to make the "holy choice." The choice of holiness sets the stage for the next event and is the system that affects my destiny. I say "affects" rather than "determines" my destiny, as there is another field of influence involved—the field of Grace, mother of Gratitude.

To accept my sensitivity as a valid defense system against a spiritual mistake, rather than a something that keeps me from having a "good time" was a milestone. This acceptance helped me love myself better and began the awareness I have been studying—the presence in this world of two zones of spiritual activity—the Zone of Holiness and the zone of profanity. As I study and experiment with trying to define "holy" I understand more about my past and why I felt as I did at certain times. I understand the choices I made in the past. Some of the past cell memory comes up for cancelling and sending to the trash bin. Some is destructive and some simply unnecessary. A way to live without the baggage of the past we don't need, is explored here in the chapters that follow.

Now, when I find myself in a zone that feels profane, I quickly and quietly remove myself as soon as possible without apology. I now give myself permission to not do certain things I felt pressured to do in the past. I understand why the energy in those situations feels uncomfortable and know that I have good reason to stay away. The zone of profanity can be anywhere at any time. There is no list of places that are profane and places that are holy. A place that is holy at one time can be profane at another. The key to knowing which zone we are in, is the ability to note a peculiar energy that provides the information. I have experienced a true Zone of Holiness at times, then without warning it become violated by profanity. That certain sense of panic is your clue. At some of these times I was relatively trapped yet saved by Grace, mother of Gratitude. These are times of instruction. It is subtle at times and neon at others. Our job is to move out of the profane as soon as we can. This is life's most important skill. At every crossroads of choice there are two voices. To know the Advocate's voice and follow and to reject the voice of the adversary is knowledge that matters.

Here, I explore the ways I have found to know that our choices come from who we are—our holy, signature, love pattern—and not from some errant cell memory or social pressure; and how to know what to do next almost all the time. This knowing what to do and doing it, is the working part of what it means to be holy and live in the Zone of Holiness. Each one of us is holy on the soul level as creations of God. The ideal is to live in a field of energy that is holy where we are at home spiritually and physically. At first, we are dependent on others and our environment. Later, as we grow and experience life we have opportunities to become aware of the truth that we have a choice to live in holiness or in profanity.

If you sense that you are in a place of profanity, this is the red flare alerting you to move out quickly and quietly. Find a place of holiness for your spirit and for your body. The Holy Spirit of the Almighty One will open your understanding, if you want to know, and you will understand the reason for your feelings and what to do next.

Our natural tendency is to seek the holy, yet we always have a choice. Drugs, alcohol, and other addictions—even those that appear innocent such as addictions to work, food, exercise, open the door to feeling more comfortable with profanity than holiness for a time, until the damage is obvious. We enter an energy field of profanity at times through innocent distractions, something "everyone does" or an involvement that begins as self help. Self-help can turn into self-blessing, denying our access to divine blessings. When we begin to understand and recognize the look of profanity and the look, taste, sound, smell and touch of the holy, we can then name our choices as holy or profane. At this point, we have a peculiar power over the forces of evil. We can then understand that choosing profanity over holiness separates us from our own self—our original love pattern, and from our main reason for being—companionship with the Almighty One. Our reactions to the profane become dramatic. The cell water becomes acclimated to holiness and is not at home anywhere else. If the concepts here resonate with you, they will organically and automatically support you and become part of your life as you are ready.

***

A "mission impossible" was delivered to my box through an assignment to my Spirit—to find out how to live in the holy zone and why. I have the same mission now and it goes on and on. This book ends with the silent message that it is not an end but a beginning. To finish this book and publish the message, I made the choice to write and complete this project as a priority rather than something way down the road. It has required an exercise of left-brain character and some talking to myself to make that happen. Here you will find some hard logic, quiet prose and some rhapsodic flights of thought to deliver the revelations I have received.

1

Finding the Holy Zone in Everyday Life

To find something we best learn how it looks, tastes, feels to the touch, sounds and smells. We are given the five senses to help us find and choose. I use the sense of sight, taste, touch, sound and smell, plus some other senses to find the Zone of Holiness. Our physical senses are part of the spiritual journey, just as our spiritual senses are part of the physical journey.

As I lent myself to find a title for this book, loud music was playing from another room in the house: "This is the dawning of the Age of Aquarius...." I heard "Age of Asparagus." Often I read road signs this way. My subconscious provides surprise words. I pondered: "Is this is the dawning of the age of asparagus"? At first it was humorous. The song played through my mind all day until I understood it to be a message to my spirit as clear as any had ever been. The asparagus part is still amusing, yet I see signs that there *is a new day dawning* for me, for my family, my homeland and the world. We are called to a new way of being human. The tilt of life is moving from the profane to the holy, and from the overly yang energy to the balancing state of yin. When yin goes too far, then yang increases to give balance. Holiness is not yang or yin; it involves a balance of the two. There is much more to holiness than a balance of yang and yin (male and female) energies or any kind of energy. I continue to discover what and where holiness is, what it does and why. The "asparagus" part was just another clue to provide a path to guide me to the next discovery I needed. Sometimes the "clues" rationally seem remotely connected to the revelation—even random. The way I explain that loose connection is that God knows us. He knows how our minds and souls are designed and the look of our cell memory patterns. He knows what will cause us to make particular connections in the quickest way—and provides what is necessary at the right time. This is simply the way God works. The gaps in my understanding are areas of mystery that will be there until there is a need to know more.

I was reading the Bible about the same time as the asparagus thoughts were simmering. I was drawn again to read the pages of the Old Testament, King James Version. I read through Genesis and Exodus and then began to read Leviticus. The tenth Chapter of Leviticus gave me pause. When I came to the following words that are ascribed to Aaron, an Israelite Priest, I knew in my mind and heart what the title of my book was to be:

"The Lord spake unto Aaron, saying...
it shall be a statute forever throughout your generations:
And that ye may put difference between holy and unholy,
and between unclean and clean;
And that ye may teach the children of Israel all the statutes
which the Lord hath spoken unto them by the hand of Moses."
—*The Bible*, Leviticus 10:8-10

The message of Leviticus 10 was originally directed to the Israelites, yet it has become *our* mandate since Jesus—to live the difference between the holy and the profane—clean and unclean.

As our awareness evolves, *we* become priests and companions to God—the power and the glory of this relationship ever evolving as we learn to distinguish these opposite energy frequencies. The intent of this writing is to give clues as clues have been given to me, revealing the look, taste, smell, touch, and sound of the Zone of Holiness in everyday life. I am learning more every day about the difference between clean and unclean—between holy and unholy. I suspect that this learning will go on and on, towards another and another holy of holies in every part of life out even into infinity. I give you what I have now, as all we ever have is now—to leave for another or take for yourself.

Beyond making us Priests and clearing the barrier between mankind and God, the gift offered you and me through the blood sacrifice of Jesus, gives us the phenomenal option of cleansing our cell memories that record "sin"—energized negative experience held in our body cells—from our own experiences, from our ancestors and from the experience of all mankind—and explored here in Chapter Eleven. Our part is to accept the gift—believe in Jesus and receive the Holy Spirit to guide and comfort. Thereafter, with daily experience, we learn—then teach, empowered. If the idea of Jesus, the cross, cleansing cell memory, holiness and cleanliness does not resonate with you at this time, please keep reading. There is something here for you amidst any kind of doubt you may have, that will allow you to ride the wave of God's Grace until you can see clearly what to do.

***

The Spirit instructed me that there are certain foods that are holy, such as asparagus. The level of nourishment is so great for our bodies that they are set apart for special good and defend us from the curse of the profane in this world. We are given clues during our days and nights—things that the Holy Spirit (voice of God) highlights. We are wise to follow if it does no apparent harm. As we practice noticing the Holy Spirit's voice we will know whether it is from the Advocate or the Adversary. Our body energy will signal peace or disturbance. Peace indicates a message from the Advocate. Disturbance indicates that the Adversary is trying to tune us in and interfere with our progress.

When someone or something is "holy"—that person or thing is probably set apart for good purpose beyond "the curse of evil" in a sacred zone. I say "probably" because there are some vital concepts that we as human beings will never fully understand. They are in the area of God's mystery. "Holiness" is one of these mysterious words. Because of it's importance to life, I continue to use the word "holy" with whatever level of understanding I have and as the understanding evolves, acknowledging the mysterious gaps.

I suspect that many of us want to live this way—in the Zone of Holiness—whether we know it or not. I find that the opposite of "holy" is "oppressed with evil" or "cursed." The energy frequency of a "curse" is probably the root cause of many illnesses, many kinds of depression, anger, hate, violence and fear—those circumstances and feelings that foster every problem on earth. The person who is suffering the effects of this profanity may *not* be the person who caused the problem, as sin cell memory is inherited from ancestors and from all of mankind's experience. The words of the Bible in Leviticus 11 contain divine messages to mankind through Moses and the priest, Aaron to help the Israelites see the difference between clean and unclean, holy and unholy meat, to keep them out of physical trouble. Holy is not just spiritual, it is an energy that inhabits the body and all material things as well.

"For I am the Lord your God: ye shall therefore sanctify your-selves, and ye shall be holy; for I am holy."

The Bible, Leviticus 11:44

The true meaning of "holy" is something to be experienced. The concept of holiness is illusive. The essence of the term is found in its being outside of rational confines. "Holy" is often used to express a feeling that is beyond understanding—"holy molee"—"holy smoke"—"holy Moses"—"holy" anything that "blows" the mind. The word "holy" carries with it a peculiar protectiveness as being out-side the curse of evil—as far from evil as possible. If "holiness" is beyond the curse of evil, I want to be in that zone. This is my desire because I love myself. I want the other people I love to be with me in that zone. I want everyone to be there. I believe the zone of "holiness" is the zone of peace. Having a peaceful spirit rather than a troubled spirit, is something I desire for myself and for my loved ones. To live beyond the opposite of holy and stay out of trouble as much as possible, there are rules to follow; yet there is Grace. If I shut down this book writing because there are no absolutes to give you and no testimonies that prove every-thing I say, I would be errant and without virtue. Your patience in reading my delicate handling of "holiness" and "profanity" will be rewarded later in this book with some daily life "down to earth" discussion and revelations.

As we learn to be in the Zone of Holiness, and make holy choices, even if we don't know exactly what we are about, others are encouraged and empowered to do the same. The ripple effect raises life quality for everyone. With this said, I proceed with the results of my exploration.

Holiness is required of mankind at this place in time...more than before. The vibrations of a "holy difference" have begun to sound a call for those attuned. Within me, a vibration of holiness has been set in motion. Within you, if your spirit resonates with the message of the Zone of Holiness, the waves of holiness are moving to cast out the profane, even as you sleep. Mankind has begun regeneration. God has allowed man to run free, loose and full throttle—men and women testing and trying the holy and the profane for many years since the advent of Christ, author of Grace. In the Old Testament there was strict law for man to follow and strict punishment for variance. Then God's position changed, as part of a great, mysterious plan. Human understanding can only glimpse the magnitude and logic of God's continual intervention and automatic interaction with the Crown of His Creation. Our place is to watch, hear, trust, follow and enjoy.

I find it particularly interesting that there are certain things in this world that are either profane or holy, with their efficacy for raising or lowering the quality of human life—residing in *how they are used* or abused. These "things" have the electrical frequency of the color "yellow." The word "things" is one of my favorites. I use it intentionally with the poetic license granted me when I graduated from Baylor University in English and Art. Electronic technology is one of those "things" that can go either way. Technological gadgets have become an essential part of daily life for people all over the world. They can be holy or profane. We are charged with discovering what electronic technology is to be in our personal lives.

In 2014, as vibrations of holiness are beginning to move our bodies and our thoughts—at the same time we live in the age of electronic technology. This advance in communications and in electronic tool making, helps man to do what he wants to do and let it be known. However, the risk of abuse, as with any advance—is present. We find a fast and loose use of technology, for power and material gain—even for good intended purpose—too much "in our face"—too much into our personal energy fields. It has gone too far. The chronic need to defend against the intrusion of "un-human" energy fields has become epidemic, all over the world. Our subconscious, yet continual defense of our energy field causes tension. Tension causes stress, which hosts illnesses of various kinds. Electronic intrusion is likely the root cause of many physical and psychological problems people suffer. The medical solutions alone are inadequate. Energy workers are swamped. They can provide great help, but one probable cause of this stress—electronic intrusion—remains largely unaddressed. Electronic intrusion like alcohol and drugs are intruders that cause chaos in our personal energy fields. These intruders cause a person to forget who he is...to temporarily forget the original love impulses which serve to move him into the Holy Zone. A door is opened for a subtle and more destructive intrusion—the deceptive curse of evil—that which fuels profanity. Yellow energy abused becomes profanity, the seen and heard, smelled, touched and tasted opposite of holiness. Awareness and knowledge gives us power to correct and cure this abuse.

I hope to write the next book with more detachment from electronics. A voice activated computer program that types what I dictate may be the answer. Making changes and laying down thoughts is so easy with a word processor and document software. Convenience is often a trap. Electronic technology is a God given tool, but can be overused and abused. My protocol for this writing is to work at the computer for 30 minutes, then take a break with fresh air, water, sunshine and some kind of motion or singing. If I don't observe this protocol, my work suffers. If I'm not careful about where and how long I work, my work zone will become profane because of the potential for negative impact on my well-being. I drew out my copper dowsing rods and checked the place where I had been working for a couple of days straight and found the rods crossed, indicating underground stream activity that increases the intensity of the electromagnetic turbulence and the risk for intrusion into my own energy field. I changed my work location after checking the area to a place over which the dowsing rods remain parallel. I do what I can. I can't help what I don't know. Basically to work in a peaceful area is best. When I use the computer, I work for half an hour, then go outside and stir the flow of bio-electromagnetic energy within myself. In other words, I take breaks.

Many of us live with a computer on our belly and a cell phone on our hip. This is a recipe for stressing the signature energy field. Selective, intentional use of technology has taken the world to a new potential for communication, evolvement and peace—nevertheless, we are at a crossroads. *Before science discovers why*, we need to limit our exposure to electromagnetic energy fields that interfere with our own. There is research on the subject—on the internet and in books that have been published. My cell phone is a wonder and a comfort; but I try to keep it at least ten feet away from my body when not in use. I use it carefully, with scant and intentional touch. Electronics tax our energy field and immune system. They tax all systems of the body because our bodies are busy dealing with the intrusion as a priority rather than our digestion, our immunity and our self-repair. Because of our addiction to—or lean towards convenience and instant response and reward—to move into the Zone of Holiness takes intelligent awareness and commitment to our own health and quality of life and that of future generations.

Who we are and what we really want becomes known to us as the result of our daily choices when they are consistent with holiness. We are in for surprise. There is a peculiar mystery about each one of us. Only God knows our true Identity until our holy choices make it public. The definition of "integrity" is "making holy choices." The way your life looks now and mine, changes as our daily life aligns with God's holy order. There is order within order within the Holy Zone as we become acquainted with same by daily experiment, and evolve into that person we are designed to be. We are revealed undiminished, as our original love materializes.

Now—in the year 2014, for mankind to embrace the holy difference is mandatory for his preservation. *To find this zone, with the help of the Holy Spirit to guide us, and to live there is our primary job.* It can be our primary joy also. As more of us accept this responsibility, and synchronize our daily lives primarily with the energy of yin, without rejecting the balancing aspects of yang, our world will recover peace, be cleansed, refreshed and healed. Mankind will experience rehabilitation and be saved from destruction. I am called to know and follow that which is harmonious with this holiness required for regeneration. All persons that want this knowledge can receive it to the level that they are ready to take the responsibility involved. It is not always an easy road because things happen that upset us at times. Nevertheless, if our heart is towards holiness, we will evolve to live in the Zone and find peace even in troubles.

These pages contain the revelation I have received over the past seven years. I give to you in the words I know to use—a guide to gain more holiness in your daily life. A plan created *by you* for your personal living on earth is necessary. This book contains *my* plan. You are well served to create your own and use it daily. It has been said, "the devil is in the details." I prefer to say, "the Lord is in the details." When you create the Protocol of Life for yourself with details to facilitate God's laws, it creates a Zone of Holiness within and around you. Otherwise, it is easy for profanity to slip in. Because you create the Protocol, you will not *resist* it or find it stressful. The Age of Holiness is emerging to balance the Electronic Age just as yin balances yang. It will save mankind from destruction, all as planned by the Creator. I prayed to know and continue to pray for more knowledge concerning the concepts here. Educator, David Starr Jordan, born in 1851, first said, "Wisdom is knowing what to do next, skill is knowing how to do it and virtue is doing it." This book is about "what to do next" and why—sharing with you my answers to prayer.

***

Eating food is a daily need and pleasure, therefore a major part of our existence on earth. I am grateful for the value of food in everyday life. The Zone of Holiness in certain foods or foods in the Zone of Holiness help to keep us, hold us, charge us, and set us apart for good purpose, protected from the curse of evil (the destructive influence of Satan). Asparagus, apple, avocado, apricot, berries, coconut and the moringa tree are a few of the hundreds of holy foods. I take food "supplements" made from the rainforest botanicals of the Amazon and a few other supplements, because I feel that I need more potent fuel than I can get where I live. Your ability to absorb and use nutrients from the food where you are—your venue—may be great enough to keep your body adequately fed without supplements. Our venue is where we are placed by Universal providence, for good reason, known to us as revelation is required.

Mankind was given the gift of choice and he chose knowledge as in the story of Adam and Eve in the Bible. With knowledge comes responsibility. In the morning I know things. At night I know nothing. Knowledge is for our use in following the Spirit. In the daytime, I have work to do. At night my only responsibility is to sleep; therefore knowledge is not necessary. To keep our knowledge faculty pure and holy, we check it by the Spirit. If what presents itself as "knowledge" is not harmonious with the Advocate Spirit that is present with us to guide the materialization of our love, it cannot be trusted. It is not how much we know, but how much we know that *matters*.

Often our cell memory is contrary to the Advocate, Holy Spirit of God and must be discharged of energy and cleansed. Our cell memory contains the experiences held in our bodies from all our past experience, the past from all our ancestors and all of mankind. This is not automatically wisdom or trustworthy knowledge. As we learn to cleanse and purify the cell memory into harmony with our original love pattern received at birth, we acquire wisdom and true knowledge. We become trustworthy for more potent daily assignments that raise the quality of life— ours and all we touch. Chapter Eleven—next to last—contains a discussion of how and *why* we can cleanse our cell memory in order to be present and holy and who we are in the moment of now, and make choices that are harmonious with our purpose.

When we take in pure nutrition and our bodies are not burdened with cleansing and elimination of toxins, we are in the best position to pursue deepr levels of cleansing such as cell memory. Information exists to confirm the value of particular foods, and we have access to it easily with the internet available to people all over the world. More than the dawning of "The Age of Asparagus" and other holy foods, it is the dawning of a new way of life for all people. There is an upswing of awareness because of the global sharing of information and insight. It is this dawning—of the age of holy food and all other forms of holiness that will create a regeneration of America and the world. I am speaking of spiritual light, being at the same time, aware of spiritual darkness that exists. To go into and detail the problems of the world, unless we are compelled by necessity, only gives energy to the negative.

Some are given the responsibility to act with regard to particular, difficult situations. They have been prepared to handle them. If your name is on one of these jobs you will be given the resources, with prayer, to deal with what it involves. Our daily supply of energy is for handling only our own responsibilities.

I was "assigned" to research the holy food, asparagus. Not a difficult task in this day. I knew it was an important food, but wanted to know more. I went to the internet looking for information. Within thirty minutes I found all the confirmation I needed plus clues for the next revelation. *Fields* of asparagus are farmed in the State of Michigan. Asparagus also grows easily in Israel, Peru, California and Hawaii. I discovered that asparagus has been cultivated and eaten as a revered food for thousands of years. The high-density level of nutrition in asparagus ranks the plant near the top in value to mankind. It has *anti-inflammatory* compounds. Eating asparagus every day or so is one of the healthiest dietary choice you can make. Asparagus is in the category of "holy foods." Something or someone holy is set apart for special good, and functions beyond the curse of evil. The research on asparagus shows that it has an unusually high amount of the beneficial compound Glutathione, a chemical that protects the integrity of the cells in our bodies. As mentioned herein before and worthy of repetition...other foods in the "holy" category include coconut, moringa oleifera, apricot, avocado, tomatoes, nuts and berries. There are many others. Some of these mentioned are available to me where I live. We have here in Louisiana, an abundance of pecans, blueberries blackberries and tomatoes. I order from web stores—coconut milk powder, coconut oil and other things I consider holy that are not available in local stores or markets.

According to the authority of the Advocate Voice that quietly speaks to my Spirit: if you have holy food often, prepared with love, follow your personal holy daily regime or Life Protocol (discussed here in subsequent Chapters), read the books and writings of persons who seek the holy way versus the profane, and converse with those who want to live in a way that is set apart for good purpose—you are in a good position to overcome much of this world's deception and degrading. The force of evil is bound to lose energy against you. You are probably living in the Zone of Holiness and Automatic Good. You are in sync with Universal laws and rhythm. Daily life—now—not somewhere in the past or future, is where our life is shaped. Small passionate choices make the difference in our life and in our world.

The following Chapters offer you the basics to make holy choices in the present moment. Many people already live in the holy zone and are teaching others from their experience. You may be one of these. Words are symbols and useful to express love and holy intentions, but actions are convincing. May you be adept at both.

2

My Story

From the beginning of my awareness, about age fourteen, I searched for Jesus in every face. I didn't consciously know I was doing this. I believe I was looking for me, too. With a gift for portraits, I drew faces in my spare time and at school when class was slack. In every face, a lively spark came into the picture. The portraits were short on structure, but the Spirit was potent. I knew there were bones in faces, angles and planes, flesh and blood, but I had little interest in presenting them except as they carried the Spirit of the subject. I continued to search. There was high school, college, graduate school, law school, marriage, children, practicing law, and endeavors to take care of myself with limited knowledge. I continued to be inspired as I read the works of wonderful souls who wrote about their revelations. I was moving along and alive, but did not really know what to do in *daily life* to have freedom from stress and freedom to efficiently materialize my love. Without a clear idea of what I best do and when, I was vulnerable to all the tricks of the Adversary that cause stress. This "not knowing what to do next" is our primary stress. The lack of freedom to express our love, for whatever perceived reason, is secondary. Love finds a way. Stress, however, diminishes the entire process and is not necessary. In the background, usually, was the continued search for Jesus. I believe that we are designed to search for Him. This search takes unusual turns, depending on our cell memory and the culture we live in, but the search goes on for everyone. Back at the Ranch, I still did not know what to do with confidence beyond the apparent necessities of life. This was not acceptable to me and a tension persisted as I did many things I thought were expected of me by others, by society, and by my own self. I had stress but could not see my options at the time. "Understanding our Options" is a life study course that best be taught to children from age twelve. But who could teach it?

***

Eventually, what seemed to be an inner Voice, told me there was a way to live that was different from what appeared around me—a structure. I intended to find that *apparatus*. The journey consciously began in 2002 when I made plans to take a family vacation with myself, husband Jim, and son Nicholas. The other children were doing something else at the time. I almost backed out of the trip, as my plans seemed so outlandish at night. I found a place in the Pacific Northwest on Quadra Island, part of British Columbia, Canada, in the Strait of Georgia. The advertisement was for an "organic farmstay" at Bold Point estate. Full meals were available. It sounded perfect, but different from anything I had ever done before and further away from Louisiana than I had ever ventured. The day before leaving I almost cancelled for fear of the unknown. Nicholas had no qualms and insisted we go ahead as planned. I had no good reason to back out so the three of us flew to Vancouver, rented a car, ferried over to Parkville on Vancouver Island, then drove up the coast to the Ferry that took us to Quadra. From there, the network of strong pioneering people with a like search as mine, began to appear.

The week we spent on and getting to and from Quadra Island is one of many stories waiting to be told. Rod and Geraldine, our hosts on Quadra Island in their elegant, rustic farm home were living in a way that was close to something I was searching to find, without a name. I knew I was looking for a new way to live that was authentic and pure, but at the time, I had no conscious idea that it was the Zone of Holiness. Even after the visit, I returned to much the same life as I had before, but the spark I noticed when I was on Quadra Island remained with me. I wanted something I found in the way Geraldine and Rod were living, yet I wanted more—something I could share with the entire world that would heal hurt and confusion and give hope to all of mankind for a better life and a better world, not just for me and my family. I kept searching, more or less quietly, pondering it all and writing in my journal.

***

My nervous system causes me to process more than is comfortable. My filters are minimum. Avoiding rules, I wanted no structure to my life than the bare minimum for fear of being someone other than me. I was searching for a way to be Authentic before I knew the word existed. I blushed when Authenticity was missing and I said or did something false—or my solar plexus would go into a tense grab. One day after the Quadra Island trip, amidst this unsatisfactory mode of living, something happened or I heard something that made me conscious of my need for a system of rules—a daily protocol. I needed guidelines to simplify my choices. The structure, however, had to be *personal* and specific to me—something I created. My anxiety level was too high—from the simple lack of the right kind of limitations. I wanted better sleep. I wanted more joy and laughter. I wanted to sing and dance and shout. I wanted to earn some money doing something I loved, and travel. I wanted to build a little ecosystem to bring children into and teach them with visuals, sound, taste, smell, and the experience of touch, how magical it is to live in harmony with Nature. To reach these goals I need structure and focus. No more sitting on the sidelines. It was time to materialize some dreams. I wanted to write a book and give to the world what I have received and more. I wanted my children to know everything that has been revealed to me, take it, and go further.

This exuberant materialization required a different way of life. A different way of life required some rules. I like things simple. I wanted some clear and simple rules to follow to prevent the waste of time and energy that happens when we have to continuously re-think our actions day and night. The rules could not be anything arbitrary or expedient; they had to be divinely inspired. I wanted to make the rules but I also wanted them to be approved by the Creator. I found it was not so much about "making" rules as it was about "discovering" them. Later I under-stood that we discover God's laws and make our rules to facilitate them. This was the harmony I sought.

I wanted to make my list of rules, yet I wanted them to be so right that if I understood them to be well founded, observing them would be an easy choice. I wanted my rules to guide me, even beyond the curse of evil. I prayed for God to show me the way. At first, when I began to think and pray about personal rules, the idea of holiness and living in the zone of automatic good had not been revealed to me. This concept appeared after my entire Protocol for Life had evolved into words, even in this book. When I was not able to meet the deadline for entering this book in a nonfiction contest because of three strange events—the "Zone of Holiness with automatic good and opposite zone of profanity with automatic evil" concept materialized. I learned that there is a real difference—not just a different way of perceiving things as some current authors insist. Later I would be shown the "Blessings Game."

All the concepts of this book are integrated into one human tendency: Our attempts to "fit in" and conform to the expectations of others, arise from the desire to avoid acknowledging the great difference between the holy and the profane and follow the call of holiness. This *great denial* is our stress. The fear of holiness and what it may entail is a device of the evil one used to great effect, particularly as the option to conform and go along with the crowd is easy and often times sparkling. To resist God actively is to engage the profane—which takes us outside the Zone of Holiness and our automatic good. Then, only God's grace, intervention and prayer is a refuge from the effects of evil.

I knew that I had to face the fear I had always with me: that I would not "fit in" to this world—that I would be different. The difference had to be *embraced*. No more resistance. Resistance was causing most of the stress in my life and I was done with it. Resistance had caused me some harm. Stress was just the sign. I prayed and found the structure I sought to make resistance unnecessary, and lower my stress at the same time. Once we ask God the right questions, everything opens us to serve our needs to know. When we know, we can go forward with abandon. Going forward with abandon in the flow with God is automatic joy and peace—and health. I began to claim the blessings of those words "automatic" and "holy" even before I was aware of the "Blessings Game." The title, The Zone of Holiness: Living Beyond our Means was a result of embracing the idea of being and living with a difference. It took seven years to find a title for this book. When we allow the automatic good to happen instead of constantly working to bless ourselves, we live beyond our means in expected, but still surprising, abundance.

***

The stress of being different is now a picnic compared to the stress of having no Protocol to follow. I see this new way of life as the Zone of Holiness. I describe here in the following chapters, the path originally designed for mankind's highest level of health and happiness. It is classic and it is *holy*. The Holy Zone in its difference to the zone of profanity, flies in the face of evil because it is greater than evil and opposite. Holiness is a zone of energy created by God that invites every one who desires to see their love efficiently materialize. The Life Protocol described here is my way to get there, and can be yours too. My success is not constant, but as I practice, I see this system of laws and rules peel off layers of stress and raise the quality of my life every day and night.

***

Being dissatisfied with the "medical" approach to being well that I experienced and noticed in the experience of others, I was drawn to energy work. The modality of Acupressure promised a way for me to take care of the condition of my body on the basic level of energy, the stuff we are made of. It promised to take me beyond the Yoga I practiced. With Acupressure I could use my own hands in a light dual station touch/hold to release energy blocks in my body. When my energy flowed with freedom, I suspected that everything would work as designed. The human body is masterfully made to self-repair. As caretakers of our body we are charged with the duty to keep it clean, well nourished with pure, fresh food, and do what is necessary to assure the free flow of energy. Acupressure is about facilitating the natural flow of personal energy. .

My own sense of good nutrition led me to choose high quality, fresh and intensely nourishing food when I had the opportunity. I always knew we best grown our own. My grandfather "Pappy" had a large garden in the nineteen fifties on rich soil that was formerly a cotton field. Hopefully pesticides were not used on the cotton or if they were, the stuff was neutralized before our vegetable garden produced! I "helped" Pappy with the work. There are pictures to prove it. I had good food as a child, but it was not enough for the life quality I desired. I needed more—searching as young as I can remember.

My Uncle Bill, the handsome man who married my mother's sister, Rosalie, was an energy worker. He studied chiropractics in the forties and practiced his art at a time when it was *illegal* in Louisiana. His sign read "William Norris, Jr.—Scientific Masseur" for years until the chiropractors sued for a right to practice their healing arts and won. Uncle Bill's eyes were opened to the value of removing obstacles to the flow of energy, when as a fourteen year old he fell out of a tree and injured his neck. His dad rounded up a local chiropractor to help him when nothing else was working. The story is that after the chiropractor performed a simple adjustment on Bill, relieving the stuck energy, he began to eat, sleep and heal. From that time on, the young man was turned in the direction of becoming a chiropractor himself. The lights had come on early for him. Growing up and "going to Uncle Bill" for help was a magical experience for me. On one such occasion I asked him why the same complaints kept coming up for him to adjust. He said, "Linda, you are just thinking wrong about something." The power of thought and belief to affect the body had been introduced to me for the first time.

It was almost thirty years later when I considered the possibility of learning the art of Acupressure, which is akin to chiropractics. I had limited my own ability to take care of myself, by the perception that energy work was for someone else. I went to law school instead, at a time when I didn't know Acupressure existed. The Chiropractic modality was too physical to draw my interest, other than to receive the benefit at times. I couldn't really think of myself as a lawyer, but I had to do something. I didn't know what to do. My Protocol at that time was to have as little limitation and structure as possible. It is a miracle I graduated, passed the bar examination given in New Orleans, was "sworn in" and practiced law for 28 years. I learned something about Protocol during this time. I took some comfort in the laws of the land, but only because they were my tools of the trade and provided some expectations for navigating. I needed something more personal.

In 2005 at the age of sixty-two, while searching the internet for a place to "live closer to nature", I found the tiny Lasqueti Island, located in the Strait of Georgia, off the coast of Vancouver, in British Columbia. I read that the four hundred permanent Lasqueti residents had rejected the Canadian electricity grid, and were protective of their ecosystem. The Canadian government had deposited posts and wire on the Island to force them to conform to the government's plans for electricity on Lasqueti. The residents did not want wires and poles on their beautiful island. The posts and wires were cut by the residents and used to make fences. The government withdrew their plans. The place drew my interest.

Curious about the Island, I read some websites that gave me more information. I noticed one Lasqueti based website offering a course of study there in Jin Shin Do° Acupressure. I had seen an Acupressure chart in a chiropractor's office one day and found it intriguing. Having an interest in Acupressure and in this small Island, I contacted the teacher and began to make arrangements for the trip. I had some fears and wondered if this was the right path for me. I prayed. I talked with the teacher's wife. She sounded gracious and reassuring. Lodging and vegetarian meals would be provided at the teacher's home. Son Nicholas, on summer vacation from college, agreed to go with me. This was the green light I needed. We made our plans to travel to Lasqueti Island, British Columbia for a basic course in Jin Shin Do°.

Nicholas and I set out to camp all the way from West Monroe, Louisiana, using my 2004 black Titan Truck, but a deluge of rain stopped us cold in Mesquite, Texas. It rained so hard we had to stop at a motel and take refuge. While unloading we saw that our truck bed cover had leaked and the camping equipment was soaked. We took a break to think it over. Nicholas got up early the next morning and missed breakfast to get on the motel computer. He asked me if he could buy us an airline ticket to Vancouver. I saw no other option and agreed.

My first son, Bach, lived in Denton, Texas, near Dallas, at the time. We were blessed to stay with him until the airline ticket arrived and the time was right to fly. He drove us to the airport and expertly escorted us through Dallas Fort Worth Airport. On we flew to Vancouver, Canada. Somehow we arranged to take a small plane and fly over the Strait of Georgia to Vancouver Island, then ferry back out to Lasqueti where we spent ten interesting, inspiring and exhausting days off the grid, learning a new to us, ancient, health promoting skill from a master teacher, Tolling Jennings. After three (3) days of class we told Tolling that we were "overwhelmed" and needed a break. He said, "Good, you should be overwhelmed." We had half a day to "walk about" but showed up at the house for supper. The ten days on Lasqueti produced some potent stories of people and things that I wrote in my local church newsletter and some I didn't write. Tolling Jennings was and is a man of integrity and Protocol, who expected the same of everyone. Nicholas and I tried our best to notice and observe the mostly unspoken rules there, but life on Lasqueti was different from life in West Monroe, Louisiana. The first rule we learned was to remove our shoes at the door and wear socks or slippers inside. I was first introduced to those plastic, clog-like shoes with holes in them that everyone wore on Lasqueti. Later, when I was home, I bought a pair of red ones like Tolling and Kay wore every day outside.

During some "down time" between classes Nicholas and I walked a bit around the place then headed back. One morning we were on the footpath leading to Tolling's home where we stayed, and saw him up ahead, taking an outdoor shower next to the "holy" sauna. We didn't know whether to go back to the road and wait, say "hi" or just walk on by and not look. We chose the latter.

Before our Acupressure workshop began, there was a wedding on the island like none I had ever seen before. Everyone was invited. The reception table was spread with the bounty of local produce, bread and fish, prepared and provided by the residents. On the table was huge bowl of raspberries. We were fortunate to be on Lasqueti at the prime time for berries—blackberries and raspberries—very holy foods.

We arrived early because the rain changed our travel plans. By the providence of God we found a place to stay. Nick and I enjoyed the generous and gracious hospitality of a lovely young grandmother at her small homestead with a big barn and garden. We were there for four days before time to begin class. Our hostess was a great cook and became a good friend. We had beds in the loft of her large horse barn. I enjoyed the outside shower, screened with bamboo shades and vines and the outhouse looking onto a treed slope, although I prefer inside accommodations. My first time to experience blackberry pie was there with a family group at the kitchen table one night after supper, with whipped cream. It became my favorite.

At the island wedding, the guests danced to a twenty or so piece marimba band. The marimbas were all different sizes. The small ones were higher pitched and the large marimbas vibrated with bass tones. The islanders who were in the band, had been to a workshop there on Lasqueti Island, led by a master craftsman of wooden musical instruments. Each student had made his own marimba. I was told that these marimba players loved the experience of making their own instruments and learning simple music so much that they met and practiced together after their workshop leader left. Soon they became popular and in demand for occasions on and off the island. At the wedding celebration held after a small family ceremony, the sound of acoustical music filled the Community Hall. The four women singers held microphones and wore long dresses of colorful African style prints. They sang with exuberance in some language I did not understand; but I remember hearing "Jesus!" in one of the songs. There was a man there in a wheel chair "dancing" with his sister who was pushing the chair from behind. One elderly gentleman sat near the stage for a while and listened. The locals told me he had the senility ailment. Soon the powerful acoustic vibrations of marimba took over. He got up and began to dance by himself.

Nicholas was gracious and good to study with me, but as a young college student, his attention span to Acupressure was limited. He had to "walk about" some on the island, go down to the bay, throw the Frisbee golf disc, and think his own thoughts. We absorbed all we could of the Acupressure way of health enhancement and this new way of life on Lasqueti Island—then back to the U.S. and Louisiana, never to be the same. That was in 2005. Before we left, I asked my teacher to tell me who designed this method of Jin Shin Do° Acupressure. He told us that Iona Teeguarden created the method we studied. Was she still alive? "Oh yes" he said. "Where?" I wanted to know. After leaving Lasqueti, I began to make mental plans to visit Iona Marsaa Teeguarden and learn what I could from her. I discovered that she wrote the books: *Acupressure Way of Health, The Joy of Feeling, A Complete Guide to Acupressure* and accepts a few students each year in California. Occasionally, Ms. Teeguarden teaches Jin Shin Do° Bodymind Acupressure° classes in other states and countries.

In 2007 I packed my big black truck with everything I could possibly need to stay in an 8' by 10' tack room with a small window, on a small horse ranch in southern California for ten days. Lodging was available in one of three student houses but the tack room was inexpensive and I enjoyed the idea of being out near the horses.

Iona Teeguarden emailed me early on that we would "feed ourselves" so I packed some things for that purpose, along with my clothes, bedding, a cotton Indian blanket, a couple of rugs, two garage sale $1 lamps, a small ice chest, a big blue enamel tub loaded with kitchen items and headed for California—alone this time. By chance, it seemed, Nicholas came over from Louisiana Tech the Sunday I left to head west. He was surprised to learn the reality of my trip. I have dreams and share them with my children but when they happen, everyone is surprised.

It took me four days to get to the workshop location. I had no trouble along the way until I got to the end of a mile of unpaved road leading to the Ranch, where I turned right too soon and found myself "lost" in my truck near the top of a steep hill. Perched up there I stopped and I decided to call the number that had been provided, and one of Iona's helpers came and rescued me. From there, it was pure joy...the joy of feeling, learning and being. I am grateful to Iona Teeguarden for her work in presenting Jin Shin Do° Acupressure to my part of the world.

In 2007, fortified with Acupressure and nutrition, along with a vision for this new way of life, I began the leg of my journey that brings me here to you. The personal protocol I necessarily created for my trip to southern California served me well. I knew from that experience that Protocol was a vital part of the game of life here on earth.

Later on, in 2009, my brother in law who is a medical doctor told me about an energy worker in Carrollton, Texas who did Acupressure with a system he developed called TKM°. He was particularly interested because the man, Glenn King, was a follower of Jesus Christ openly and helped people that the medical community "gave up on" with his Acupressure-like modality of hands on, dual touch, energy moving art. I thought about it and could not stay away from going to a class the first chance I had. Husband Jim and I went to Carrollton and attended a basic level class in TKM° where I absorbed all I could process, bought the book and let it sit for a year. It seemed too much to handle at the time, so I let it alone. I was motivated at some point after a year to pick up the materials, read, and was again fascinated with the way doctor Glenn King openly credits God for everything he had become and everything he could do with TKM°. He was not worried about being currently cool. I went back to Texas alone and took another class. It was an overwhelming experience, shaking me up with the assignments my Spirit received to go home and do something with it.

I began practicing TKM° on my family and on myself, also using Jinshindo° Acupressure when the situation seemed right for it. The results were always good and often dramatic. The two modalities are from the same root science of energy—quantum physics—and from a particular Japanese gentlemen, Jiro Murai, who was "miraculously" healed from a "uncurable" disease using some memories of touch routines and finger holding patterns used to treat people from his past. Jiro Murai was from a line of medical doctors on his mother's side of the family. Murai was given some specific revelations about energy pathways and particular touch/holds that release blocked energy, all of which he meticulously diagramed after his recovery. Glenn King and Iona Teeguarden both used materials and methods from Jiro Murai to construct their individual systems that are akin, but quite different. I am thankful to the Holy Spirit for prompting me to take notice of Jinshindo° Acupressure and of TKM° for my own well being and for those I help. I recommend taking classes in both or one of these to you, as the Spirit leads. Each one—Jinshindo° Acupressure and TKM°—both powerful health modalities, have an essential protocol used in every session that is designed to produce optimal results safely, with the least effort and time spent. The discoveries continued as the material for this book was being written. My story goes on unreported, and now becomes a silent background for the revelations I have been given and give to you for making this life a materialization of your heart's desire—with the least effort, time and trouble.

3

The Power of Protocol

Protocol is what to do, when, most of the time, for reasons we don't have to rethink. It saves times, money, energy, and space. Protocol is a structure to build your life upon. Protocol keeps you out of trouble if it is based on Universal laws and your unique personal requirements. Protocol founded upon the inspiration of the Holy Spirit of God shuts out evil. Protocol is your sure defense against fear, guilt, anger, depression and physical illness. When you observe the right Protocol, the Universe supports you—when you don't—it won't. Powerful protocol is a daily practice of "holy habits."

Any protocol has a certain power. People who do all the wrong things by routine have the power of momentum. The power of protocol that works to *raise* the quality of life for everyone is created by your "holy habits." If we can change profane habits to holy ones we can make the world a better place in which to dwell—fast. Our personal life is made better—fast—by small holy habits, intentionally replacing restrictive and negative habits. This world is full of infinite beauty. There are millions of beautiful people in this world—past, present and future—people we have met and people we will meet in the future. The design is perfect, yet the challenge remains in how we manage evil (that which degrades the expression of love). Evil is dissolved by the awareness and practice of holiness. This book is an exploration into the process of finding the Zone of Holiness where love can be perfectly materialized without the curse of evil. The presence of evil is part of God's design—but our job is to learn what to do with it. Learning how to handle evil and keep it at bay with holiness, automatically transforms us into good companions to God and to each other.

All my life I have resisted rules and the over lording of other people—wanting to avoid missing what I am about by following the broad and ordinary path—the accepted and even the good path. I have resisted the chance of becoming someone else. Now, with seventy years of life experience under my belt, I realize that having a set of rules—Personal Life Protocol—is one of the most liberating and individually empowering choices we can make. Life Protocol has been the key to uncovering who I am, what I want and how to get it. The same key is yours.

This book contains almost everything I have learned in the process of searching for an efficient way to know myself, my dreams and materialize them. The parts left out of this story are negative cell memories from which I have intentionally and with prayer, discharged all the energy, to prevent them from affecting me or those I influence. I don't want to recharge them for the sake of drama.

Personal Life Protocol is effective to the extent it is created by you and for you, individually, with inspiration and instruction from God—then followed. This Life Protocol is the closet thing to good magic that exists on earth—it is Holy. You may wonder how a set of rules that a person follows each day can lead him to all this fabulous sounding goodness. It is, of course, more than a set of rules. Personal Life Protocol is a mindset and a spiritual attitude. It delivers—to the extent you apply it to your self. Your Life Protocol will be somewhat different from mine and it will work for you and change as your understanding increases. Life Protocol is fun. It gives you needed detachment in this manipulative world we live in. Many good people have problems from simply failing to find the detachment required to relax and accept themselves and where they are at a given moment. Personal Protocol creates a confident detachment, giving a person freedom and a sense of space, to think and feel in such a way that draws upon resources from the Universe.

Bring your own intelligence to bear on your personal daily needs and make yourself a structure. I admit up front that I believe there is a rhythm and a structure that all of us and each of us best consider in deciding what to do and when. We are all subject to the same basic rules of humanity, like it or not. We can try to circumvent and deny the Universal laws of life, but our resistance does not make them go away—it only causes stress and makes the work of Satan easier.

Acknowledging and using Life Protocol is the way to optimize our energy to create a satisfying and magical feeling life. Instead of limiting us, our lives become particularly and personally fulfilled by the use of structure. Instead of being discounted and limited by laws, our deepest desires are quickly revealed to us in objective ways when we follow Protocol.

***

We are all different. Some lead with the heart and others with the head. Being a rhapsodic dreamer is a wonderful way to live when balanced by an understanding of the power in Life Protocol. Being a practical no frills person gets some jobs done that we need done that someone has to do; yet if this person can catch the vision of the "Blessings Game" explored in this book, his heart's desire will manifest without planning and effort.

Our dreams and heart felt desires are turned into reality when we honor God's laws with obedience. When our hearts (spiritual center of being) are listening for guidance, there will be times when Protocol bows to an opportunity of the moment. This is the time to drop everything and go with the impulse—act upon it in love—then return afterwards, to the routine of day and night, confident that our love will ripple on out supported by Universal orchestration, and accomplish things we cannot do alone. We have followed the Holy Spirit that knows who we are, what we are about, and what forces are aligned to create a desired result. Expect to be blessed in a surprising way.

I decided one day to create a Protocol for making the holy biscuit. It was inspired. The holy way to cook is to first think of what you want, next look around and see what foods you have that are fresh and whole, or natural and unpolluted with chemicals—then consider how you can put your desires of the moment with the food you have together in a way that tastes, smells and looks wonderful. It's fun. If you feel challenged—pray for help. You can do it. My husband is accustomed to eating very unusual preparations that are healthy! There's a holy way to do everything that isn't evil. I give the biscuit recipe to you herein below. If you're not ready for Protocol, at least you will have biscuits. There's no use trying to vary the recipe because of the laws of nature and science. It simply is the best if you like rich, fluffy biscuits in a crisp rich crust, made with health supporting ingredients, particularly the holy coconut oil. If you use butter instead of coconut oil, it will be good, yet not as nourishing.

BISCUIT RECIPE

Ingredients:

1 cup organic white flour. Place an extra 4 or 5 tablespoons of
  flour in a shallow bowl for forming biscuits.
1 teaspoon aluminum free baking powder.
¼ teaspoon sea salt.
l pinch baking soda.
3 level tablespoons raw cold pressed coconut oil.
l scant cup buttermilk.

Method:

Preheat oven to 375 degrees (toaster oven is good).
Wash hands clean and dry them.
Mix dry ingredients with wire whisk in a medium bowl.
Pinch the coconut oil into the dry ingredients with your fingers.
Between your clean dry hands, coat the flour mixture with
  coconut oil by picking up hands full of the mixture and pressing
  hands together in a rubbing motion. This will take approxi-
  mately 80 rubs. Be patient and enjoy this process.
(This adds love and creates fluffy texture.)
Add the buttermilk, then lightly fold it in good with a silicon
  bowl scraper/spatula.
Use the scraper to scoop up the dough to form biscuits—this
  recipe will make five or six.
Place each scoop of biscuit dough in the flour that you set aside
  in the shallow bowl and toss it around lightly to coat. Set the
  biscuits close together in a ceramic baking dish that has been
  greased with coconut oil. Fiesta ware works perfectly—a flat
  bowl or medium sized baking ramekin.
(If you like thin crisp biscuits, simply use a "plate" size ceramic
  tart pan and pat them down and touching, to bake.)
Bake for 25 minutes or until golden brown.

There is a best way to live, just as there is a best way to make biscuits. We try to vary the recipe of our Creation and do our own thing but end up discovering these laws I am giving you are the easiest and most enjoyable way—perhaps the only way—to look, feel and live our best. Chase your tail if you wish—I did. As my good friend, Barbara, repeats often: "Our God is a God of Order!" This applies to nature—and man is not outside natural order. Human beings are designed by and subject to Universal laws—the laws of God. To be comfortable that you and I are together in our thinking, I define certain terms that defy definition:

God is the Highest Intelligence and all-powerful Creator of the Universe—the original source of Truth, Love and Life.

Love is the energy pattern and impulses of God, a part of which we are, and the creative force of the Universe.

The Devil is Satan, the permitted deceiver of mankind; the original source of hate, fear, pride, envy and lies.

Evil is the opposite of love and truth—the destructive, incoherent energy patterns and impulses of the Universe.

Good is whatever energy pattern and impulses support the materialization of love.

Bad is whatever energy pattern and impulses degrade the materialization of love.

These definitions are as precise as necessary in using words, our symbols for communicating with each other. No words can prove or disprove any of the above, as the concepts of God, Love, Devil, Evil, Good and Bad are so large they defy proof, complete definition, or disproof. They evolve with mankind—by design.

As change in your Personal Life Protocol is required by experience and inspiration, make the changes. When you experience the power of Protocol in a few areas of your life, you will find within yourself a desire for each task or adventure you approach in life to be handled according to priorities, integrity, and with the appropriate skill. You won't be satisfied with less. Try not to be a dictator in your commitment to the ideal. Kindness and relationships are more important than doing a job perfectly. Love is the highest priority—it pre-empts any set of guidelines. Love is in the energy that moves us to action. No set of rules is worth anything without Love.

Protocol is best written into words to keep the mind free for receiving and processing new life. When change is needed, make the change on paper. Refine your gold and place it in the treasure chest of your computer files or journal. This is a special gift to yourself and if you choose, to all those you love and influence.

Better than money or possessions, your Personal Life Protocol experience is a gift to those you care most about, affecting everyone you touch in this life, as you use the highest level of integrity you are capable of for its creation and management. Your Life Protocol will help keep you out of harm's way—out of the zone of profanity. All the people and resources you need to experience the glory God intends for you, will be provided.

***

God tests us in this life to determine if we are wise enough to follow His Order without understanding it completely. There is a huge reward waiting if we can. Finding our Life Protocol is accomplished by asking for divine help, listening to the right Voice, then following the clues. The history of Israel in the Old Testament book of Exodus shows some dramatic testing. The law of Moses was God given Protocol for the people of Israel at a particular time in the history of mankind. Good things happened when it was obeyed and bad things happen when the people disobeyed the Protocol.

God mysteriously, probably by design, changed His attitude towards mankind with the advent of Jesus, who provides a new "test"—the test of faith and love. Mankind was self- destructing. Everything changed with Christ. *The harsh strictness of Leviticus 10* relaxes to the Grace given to those who look to Jesus even in stumbling faith and desire to follow Him. The highest Order re- mains to live a life that is *clearly different* in refusing to be deceived by the Evil One. Perfection is not required, simply an intent of heart to follow Jesus and reject Satan. There is always Grace. I suspect the wisest among us has the human vulnerability to be fooled, yet as we make daily choices according to the Life Proto- col we have prayed for and found, the look of our life shows as a Holy Difference. This look becomes stronger and clearer from inside us to outside as we view the world, and from the outside, as the world views our difference.

Belief without full understanding, that Jesus is the Savior of mankind as claimed—linking our love with His, promises abundant life on earth and eternal life beyond. We trust in Christ for everything and follow the light He gives. This is the Protocol for eternity. We can believe something we do not fully understand, like the functional magic of our computers and telephones because we experience the way it works. Life with Jesus is the same. We are given understanding as we need it and desire it. Can we discount a promise of good that amounts to materialization of our love on earth and an everlasting life beyond, because our human minds need a limited concept we can fully understand? If so-called "Christianity" doesn't appear to work, it is because the so-called "Christians" do not understand the difference of holiness, cleanliness and the "Blessing Game." This is infantile faith totally dependent on Grace. The life of such a one lacks power and materialization of his heart's desire is a remote potential because he is still duped by Satan. I write this book to help correct this discrepancy and bridge the gap between those who believe in Jesus and those who believe in holy living but not in Him who came to take us to a level of holiness not possible before his atonement for profanity—past, present and future.

Acknowledging the Creator, whom I call God, and the human revelation of the Creator, Jesus Christ, is something that will happen sooner or later. Every knee shall bow eventually and every tongue shall confess that Jesus Christ is Lord. The Universe is designed to make that happen. That is worship. The reaching out by a human spirit with awe to the living God is his/her primary purpose, clued and confirmed by all of Nature, the original Sanctuary.

We have an inborn desire to understand the mystery of Creation, yet it will forever remain hidden. Only that part of the mystery for which we can accept responsibility, will be opened to us. All else we are privileged to simply ponder and enjoy. Jesus appeared on earth in history to help us understand and define the great love of our Creator and teach us how to live. We learn about Jesus in the Bible, a book to read every morning for optimal life experience and direction. If you miss a day's reading, even if it is just one sentence, you will miss a vital link for your personal transformation from here to all you ever dreamed of possible in life. This reading is part of my morning Protocol. We cannot predict or pre-estimate the portent of Life Protocol. As we find, record, and practice it by faith, we see the value—not before, except by intellectual appreciation. Protocol takes us to where we need to be, physically and spiritually—it manages our health, our love story, give us peace and joy and opens the flow of material resources to our lives—all without undue effort—even automatically. With Jesus as our Savior, this Protocol of faith is a structure that spirals us upward and outward with a clockwise direction of energy flow that is finer and more aware every day, into an evolvement that goes on and on for eternity.

As the Bible pages reveal the character and events in the earthly life of Jesus Christ, a confirmation resonates within. I know this person. Somehow, I was there, with Him. Somehow He is still here. We see Him in Nature, in faces along the way. The mystery of the Bible exists and will always exist beyond our human understanding. Accepting and acting on truth we cannot fully comprehend or predict, is faith. Science gives us truth that we can predict—cause and effect on a level that we can touch, hear, smell and see. This is some degree of interest and comfort. A *spiritual science* exists, but is beyond the senses of touch, smell, taste, hearing and eyesight. Spiritual laws are potent and predictable. Those that recognize and practice them consciously are using the power that creates material reality in this world. If you do not recognize and use this power, others who do—will have power over you. Not everyone is kind and loving. As I wandered this earth from the beginning, I looked for Jesus and the Zone of Holiness, without knowing what or who I was looking for. Jesus was probably the most kind and loving individual ever to live on earth. I looked for Jesus before I had ever heard His name. We are designed to search for Him.

When Jesus left our physical earth as we perceive it, a comforter and guide remained available to every soul—the Holy Spirit. I will refer to this loving and creative Spirit often herein. The Holy Spirit, our Advocate, will lead us to the understanding as we read the Bible over and over again in a never-ending search for truth. As we are ready we will understand.

Often when we understand something in life for the first time, we will notice a seed of need there—a *job* is created. When our name is on it, no one else can do it. Our job of the moment is specific to each individual. Faith is required because we cannot know why or what or when in advance or where our actions will take us or make us or how others will be affected. Faith is belief in the unseen and unproved truth that we know. At the point when we accept our job, God and the Universe sets upon the moment to infuse the acts we perform with a particular power and provide the specific resources required. We are privileged to observe. This is probably the highest entertainment man can enjoy. No television program, personal interaction, movie, book, sports event or video game can come close. Accepting personal, unique responsibility is Left index finger prompt of my Personal Life Protocol discussed in Chapter Eight. Trust your spirit to give the truth as it applies to you in your reading of this book.

***

My vision of life is offered to you now without formal proof. If I wait, study and test everything I want to say to you, the result may be diminished because of timing. There is a scripture that I enjoy in the Bible from I Corinthians 12:7 "Now, the Spirit shows Himself to each one to make him useful." In a different way each is called to contribute something to the body of Mankind. May I hear, be and do as the Spirit directs. Where my proof is lacking, your experience is present to confirm what resonates with your spirit. I testify to you of what I know and believe from my experience and revelation. I expect you to find value in this writing—something that will help you realize the desires of your heart and make them happen in a tangible way. This book is written because of a compelling need I have to do so that I do not fully understand. It is my responsibility and my personal assignment from the Creator.

All truth is locked up in mystery. Even as I write the truth perceive, I realize the mystery of the unknown extends to infinity and is within every word. Words are symbols and tools. Some mysteries are meant to stay beyond understanding. I am thankful to understand something occasionally but acknowledging mystery thankfully relieves me of much responsibility and creates detachment. Detachment is necessary to live effectively—another way of saying we must deny as much responsibility as we can, find the humor in ourselves and do the dance of life, in our own way. A free flow of energy is necessary for experiencing detachment. Your life protocol provides detachment as nothing else can do.

***

Energy blocks result when Life Protocol is denied and cause us pain in various ways. The cure for energy blocks and pain caused by taking on something (a responsibility) at an inappropriate time is one of the primary concepts I intend to deliver here.

Help for releasing energy blocks and pain directly and physically involves: Life Protocol (structured living preempted only by the Holy Spirit), hands on release of blocked energy in the body, plus the powerful addition of Voice (acoustical resonance). Our energy flow is expedited by orderly living, hands on healing and song. These three actions give relief to the tensions of thinking and feeling—relief from the intensity of Being and the stress that results when we are out of sync with natural law and Universal rhythm. Protocol, Acupressure, and Voice, all involve action. Our Protocol for daily/nightly life, our use of touch for energy flow and our song reveal what we believe. Our religion comes down to what we do, not what we think or say we believe. If we have faith, we are compelled to act on it. Faith conquers fear by demanding some kind of action. When we use Protocol we are exhibiting faith—the faith that says: "When I do this, God will do what He does and something good will happen." When we use even the simplest form of Jin Shin Do° Acupressure, the TKM° energy flow enhancement method, or the releases described here in Chapter Five, we say "My hands are touching energy and moving it to a more comfortable place and from this comfort I can easily express what God is revealing to me." To sing our song in the holy zone of vocal sound sets up a ripple of resonance all over our body and sends it out to others. The holy sound zone is explored here in Chapter Ten. Any way we can set in motion the vibrations of holiness, helps to counter the profanity that offends all that we love.

As discussed in Chapter Eight here, part of the Personal Protocol of Life is taking responsibility bearing our name. This observance opens the door for integrity and authenticity to happen in a personal, physical, immediate way. Group integrity and authenticity is only possible when the individuals involved personally accept nothing less. Growing up actually means taking responsibility. Anyone who does this is growing up, at any age. Once we decide to grow up and take responsibility there is a reward, but only if we use responsibility properly and deny all responsibility that is not specifically assigned to us, me—you, individually. Sometimes when a person decides to grow up (quite a moment) he or she will *over-correct* and take on everything. If we take on someone else's responsibility, or accept our own without Protocol, we invite guilt and anger. Guilt—because we can never do everything right all the time at the same time and anger because we are not having any fun.

Protocol gives us something to do or not do with confidence—to counter anxiety and idleness, both of which produce fear and guilt and all kinds of negative, useless feelings. If we ever intend to "grow up" the right Protocol is essential.

It was a happy day when the light came on for me that my life would be less stressful if I had a schedule specially designed for myself, in order to know what to do at certain times of day when there was no immediate inspiration. I gave myself permission stop carrying around everything I needed or wanted to do wondering every moment what on this huge list of 500 things I should do next. With a daily structure of chronological do(s), we always know at least generally, what to do next and have good reasons that we remember when necessary, in a journal, or somewhere handy, *why* we best do a certain thing at a particular time of day or night. We don't have to remember all the reasons and justify what, when and why every time we set out to do something. We simply remember the easy list of Do(s) and Don'ts, follow the rules, and trust them because they are prayed over, well thought-out and inspired. With rules of the day and night within our Personal Protocol of Life, we are able to turn loose of oppressive guilt that hangs around what we should or should not be doing and the fear of not measuring up to the standard of someone, our own self, or some system.

The dialogue can be heard as a part of a conversation with our Self:

"This is what I do at this time of day or night and I don't have to do anything else. In fact I best not do anything else unless the Holy Spirit gives me a command."

A suggestion by the Holy Spirit is basically a Cosmic Command. How exhilarating to have a Cosmic Command to handle. With an order from the Holy Spirit (the Voice of God), we can be assured of adequate power and resources! We are not even responsible for the results. The key to a guilt free life is following the Holy Spirit to the highest level of our ability and integrity, then letting go, trusting God to use our efforts as only He can and to do what only He can do. We may be fortunate enough to see the results of our faith and gain confidence in the process. Joy is somewhere in this also. Peace comes along with hearing, following, letting go and trusting. These are feelings no amount of money can buy—feelings that happen *automatically*. The daily rules of our Life Protocol are the default setting we have for the times when we do not hear a Cosmic Command. When we Do a certain thing at a particularly time every day and refrain from the Don'ts we are free for the Universal good to be spontaneously worked out in us with all the unlimited resources of God.

Each person is accountable to develop his/her own Protocol

with the help of clues provided by others and with the inspiration from God. The written Protocol of an individual is a list of orderly actions to do and to not do in the 24 hour time frame we have to work with, that coincides with the universe, eliminating the need to constantly re-think life and what to do with each day and night. Protocol frees me to laugh and be spontaneous as a child. As an example to allow you to see what I am doing close-up, I include here my Personal Protocol Do(s) and Don'ts. The Do(s) were developed over a year or so of noticing what order seems appropriate and what order works best each day in a natural way. Listening to the advice of God's Spirit and taking notice of my own body and spirit's needs and reaction helped me create the Do(s). The Don'ts are another story that I tell in Chapter Six. Your Do(s) and Don'ts may be quite similar to mine or different. My lists are given here to entertain and encourage your own truth to emerge when the time is right.

4

The Do(S) of Life

Part A: The Basics

When you develop a list of things to do daily that is your very own, you will not resist it. There will be no stress in following this Protocol because you create it. We do not make Universal laws as they structure all human life, but we *do* make the rules that are very personal to implement it. When you find the universal laws of your life, then add your own rules, much of the stress of resisting other people and their agendas will disappear. Stress wastes your energy and is not necessary. The following Do list is mine. I believe it is good for everyone but it is ultra important for you to *work out your own Protocol*. It will vary from mine because our gifts, our bodies and our purposes are different.

1. Awake with the Dawn. I find that awakening from sleep at dawn, doing the energy balancing while still in bed, along with a bit of meditation, is essential to start to each day. Rising at dawn is a universal principal for mankind's well being. Things go better when we do it. To ignore this principal means we spend the day compensating for the loss of time and rhythm. The resulting syncopation takes more energy than necessary to get back into the swing of the Universal ebb and flow. In a word, stress happens when we ignore Universal laws. When we get up early with the sun, we have the Universe to do much of our work for the day. We get more done with less effort. At times I sleep late but it is usually because I've been up in the night.

The energy of early morning is something special. To miss it, is to be deprived of a gentle nurturing (sunrise pink) that no other time of day provides. The sunrise itself is a spectacular reminder that there is an Intelligence and Beauty over all the world and we are part of it. To awaken at the break of dawn is ideal. I sit up, reclining comfortably with the light of dawn and listen. The sounds of morning are enchanting if you live in a quiet place. If you don't live in a quiet place, you can choose to do so. It's like waking up to music, but better. I never, if at all possible, wake up to an "alarm"—heaven forbid. If necessary, a small clock radio positioned ten feet or more from my head will do fine set on a pleasant station that plays respectful music in the early morning. One of my best experiences waking up to music was in 1971 while in New Orleans for the Louisiana bar exam (law). I stayed at an old house/hotel on St. Charles Avenue for the enduration. The vintage location and all it's timeless appeal helped balance the high pressure and cramming. I set a clock radio to come on at 6:00 a.m. tuned in to an early morning radio program. Every morning the clock radio came on at 6:00 a.m. quietly broadcasting—"In the jungle, the mighty jungle, the lion sleeps tonight....wemmboway, wemmboway..." and on it played with the primitive sounds and beat. I couldn't have chosen a better nudge to get up and study. The "jungle" was my world and I had to learn it's ways. The dawn and morning bird songs wouldn't have been enough because of what awaited me and I knew it. I wake up thankful now that I don't have to do anything but my assignments from God. The Louisiana Civil Code is another's task to learn and use.

Before descending my bed, while reclining and comfortable, I adjust my energy, releasing the blocks and congestion of energy I may feel with dual touch energy flow sequences described in Chapter Five following. I also enjoy meditation, prayer, vocal sounds (singing) and water—always water. I often wake up with tension somewhere. I named the Chapter Five energy flow sequences in a way that describes how they feel and their significance to me. The location on the body with the colors and sounds of the Releases described here have some correlation with the seven energy reservoirs of the body called "chakras" in eastern energy science. The point of the Releases is to have them available to you, easy to use and remember, and effective to help your body, mind and spirit. I find that visualizing a color associated with each of the seven main releases, and singing the sound suggested, is a good way to remember what to do and what it does for me. The singing of a sound in what I call the "Zone of Holiness" is an important part of each release. When the voice drops into the resonant "Zone" the release begins to happen *immediately*.

I have found inspiration for these special meditative, hands on Releases, from all my studies, particularly my study of the TKM° energy flow enhancement modality and from my study of Jinshindo° Acupressure. The studies and the practice of these have given me insight. I am grateful for the work that has gone before me by Iona Marsaa Teeguarden in creating Jinshindo° Acupressure and Glenn T. King in creating TKM°.

I have drawn from all my sources of inspiration, yet the daily revelations from God are my best and most honored resource. I have experimented, researched, and prayed. My purpose is to give you seven Releases that address basic needs of the body for energy balancing and flow in the simplest manner possible. Through these seven sequences, you will be introduced to the power of dual point touch for moving stuck energy, making way for the body to self repair as it was designed to do. All the following Releases are presented in Chapter Five here. They are given an entire chapter because I discuss each one in some detail. Each of these Releases helps dissolve the resistance felt as stuck energy and allows the energy to flow again. All of them help release the powerful center of the body, the solar plexus. When the solar plexus (diaphram/stomach) area of the body is free and relaxed, it helps everything else to work right.

***

When there is time, desire, and/or special need, the **Ten Finger Friends Meditation** is next in order and begins the day with a sense of readiness. This meditation is something anyone can do for help at any level of need and awareness. Words do not describe it adequately. Only by the experience can one know the true value of this meditation. Ten Finger Friends Meditation is calming and prompts an awareness of what we need to know right now. It reminds me of everything my life is about, finger by finger, with a brief expense of time. Glenn King, the originator of TKM® teaches that the fingers are directly correlated to all functions of body and all these functions total One Hundred and Forty-Four Thousand. The details of Ten Finger Friends Meditation are here in Chapter Eight.

***

After all or some of the above, my day begins by stepping out of bed into my black wool slippers and a lightened black, cotton knit robe. Son Nicholas gave it to me for Christmas this year to replace the old one I enjoyed for years that was faded and hole-y black...quiet, soft and light from one thousand or more washings. There is no synthetic material or blend of any kind in my robe or slippers. They accompany my morning energy quite well. After visiting the "necessary room" I gently apply a cloth made warm (hot) with some of the water I am boiling to heat my coffee cup and add to the mega strong espresso. Here recently, I use moringa oil mixed with a drop of peppermint oil and some mandarin orange oil, as a morning "anointment." My face seems to like it. Applying the same to my neck, arms and legs, helps to open the energy centers of my physical self and my spirit. My grandmother, Mama Nancy, would say "Glory Be!" The anointing of oil is an ancient and holy health practice for body, mind and soul.

If you care for and nurture yourself physically and spiritually, it is easy to do the same for others. I believe moringa oil is purifying and nourishing to the skin, at the least. It is said to be the finest oil in the world. After seeds are pressed to extract the oil, the hulls are used to purify water for drinking.

I am thankful for my energy and the new day. The sky seems to says "Good morning!" and "I love you" quietly and with all the power and confidence of the Universe behind it. The glory of morning comforts me. It is something I claim every day as an affirmation of God's resurgent Love. The stage is now set and my costume is in order. My early morning garb is usually blue jeans or old cotton pajama pants and a white, cotton men's T-shirt. Men's T-shirts are made better than women's and are less expensive. They are softer, longer and have a more comfortable neck and sleeve. It's not difficult to find a men's T-shirt in one hundred percent cotton, but somehow the manufacturers believe women's clothes must have a synthetic for marketing purposes. I won't go there because I have too much to say. To dress always in natural, unblended materials such as cotton, is harmonious with personal energy and encourages the flow. Anything I can bring into my personal environment than is natural, rather than synthetic, I do. Synthetics cause energy incoherence and I need all the coherence I can get.

2. Tea or Coffee Alone. Simply sitting in the presence of God and all Creation with no pressure to do anything but have coffee or tea is a reward beyond price for rising with the dawn. After my coffee (I like organic espresso coffee with heated cream and raw sugar) I read and write. Anyone can write after having a cup of rich espresso with cream and sugar! I often begin by reading the Bible because of the powerful, unexpected messages I receive when I do. Other books that I find for inspiration I also read when there is time. I usually have several of them going at once. The morning is a time of day when God's spirit speaks most clearly to my heart. I revel in this time. I recommend that you keep a daily journal and write anything you feel or think in the morning. The journal is where you can be honest completely and self-centered without guilt. If it's not self centered, I venture it inauthentic. It's your place to be vulnerable. It is necessary to journal. From about twelve years old on, children benefit powerfully from writing in their daily diary. Dare to dream unlimited dreams in the early morning when all things are possible. God confirms your dreams and prompts them. I think God enjoys tempting you with amazing dreams to see what you will do. If you actually rise with the dawn, you will feel no pressure to hurry or cut short any rhapsodic expression that these dreams inspire.

This is free time that cannot be bought or ordered online for any amount of money.

3. **Rhapsodic response.** This is the time I do something a bit wild in response to what the Spirit suggests in this new day—spending no more than about 15 minutes. Rhapsodic expression is doing something harmless that expresses love without allowing rationality to cramp it. No one else need ever see it or know about what you do at this time of the morning. I follow my heart and do something, even if it is very small. Small to us may be big to God.

4. **Body work.** I give attention next to my physical body. I prepare it to accept and support the activities that are next, usually a full day of action, nourishment and work. This rule is difficult because we are inspired sometimes to do a work early in the morning. Nevertheless, I try to never do a special project without first doing bodywork. Bodywork is best done *before* special project work to allow a better quality of energy to be used for creative and productive work. Basic health is served to release tension before focusing mind and muscle on a project. We feel better doing concentrated activity after our bodies are tuned, old energy released, fed with living food, and we are clean—in that order. Basically, it keeps down stress. Everything in the Universe has a best order of doing and being, including man. We are wise to recognize and observe this truth. The bodywork has to be fun or at least pleasant, or I won't do it. I begin my workout with vocal practice. I sing for a few minutes, no more than thirty using the principles of a voice coach I "purchased" on the internet and some visualizations and principles I have found that work for me. It is

valuable time spent and is slowly making a difference in the way I handle speaking and singing.

Next, I jump on a mini trampoline for five minutes to move energy. It is said that two minutes on the rebounder clears the lymphatic system of our bodies. Next, I use a large, inflated blue ball to balance and bounce, do easy push-ups, stretches, and bends. This ball work is fun. I cover it with a wool or cotton throw when it is cold. When the weather is nice, I greet the day with the series of stretches I learned on Lasqueti Island called the Chinese Eight Silken Movements. They work to open the energy stations of the body. Any other kind of bodywork you enjoy can be done if there is time. The practice of Yoga is a fine way to tone the body and relax tensions in a pleasant way. Yoga facilitates the release of toxins from the body. It is an ancient health and beauty practice. There is a spiritual component also in Yoga that helps reduce anxiety. If you are drawn to do Yoga, pray to find a good teacher who can help you do the poses correctly then practice alone or with a group—whichever way best fits your personality.

The practice of Yoga or whatever you prefer to call it—stretch and flow—holy maneuvers—has been used for thousands of years. It is a form of Universal body prayer that gives strength, tone and peace. Your body will thank you for doing Yoga. It will help to bring out your natural beauty. Men, this is for you too! All this bodywork takes about an hour. When there's time or a pleasant day, I walk in the park. I do what time allows after the essential things that don't take long such as the bounce and "Chinese Eights." Our seasons, the demands of the day and time naturally vary the bodywork. The bodywork is for us, not us for it. Be gentle with yourself and grateful for the ability to do anything.

5. Shower, breakfast, and dress. After bodywork, I take a filtered shower, then dress as simply as possible for the day, unless there is some occasion that has a dress code I want to observe. I don't go out much because I lack the desire to observe dress codes. My clothes and shoes must be ultra comfortable and of natural materials. My grandmother Emma who was a "beautician" would say, "suffer to be beautiful" with a scented smile. I never bought that one. She didn't suffer much to be beautiful, born with all the accoutrements of female appeal—soft pale skin, bright brown eyes, a perfectly oval face, high brows, strong nose, a well shaped mouth and a twinkling sense of humor. Emma said her husband told her she had a "million dollar figure." She got me down on the bed one day when I was about twelve and "plucked" my eyebrows. She said they made me look mean the way they were. Holy Smoke! I needed an advocate as a child. The other grandmother, Mama Nancy, nurtured me but kept quiet. Once and a while when she had had enough of something she would say "Tarnation!"

I had enough of polyester one day. I never felt good in it but didn't know why. Now I can say "No" to synthetics and know why. I avoid wearing metals and clothing made of synthetic materials or blends, which interfere with the body's signature energy field. Other things we depend upon these days, such as cell phones and computers, also interfere. If you must wear a belt, try and find something that is natural without metal components. Anything that distracts your energy at the solar plexus level is particularly offensive. The corset is probably a material item created by the energy of the "devil"—the pride and ego of women who value a popular "look" over health and comfort, and of the men who look upon women as objects for their pleasure and social status. I shiver to consider the anger cell memories that must have been generated by the corset that I have stored in me from my ancestors; and that I am required to discharge before coming to the moment in holy fashion to receive its blessings. Mother Nature is strong and benevolent, but she has limits of tolerance. The expression "when Mama is not happy, nobody is happy" has a ring of truth through the ages. Our power seat of personal energy best be uncompromised. I have long ago left off snug belts, panty hose and girdles. I wear nothing tight or restrictive for me to resist. My energy flow is vital. When my energy flows, I help those around me to flow. When it doesn't, I best be out of the way.

***

The shower—the blessing we have to wash away discharged cell memory—is better taken after bodywork, rather than before, for other reasons than just the obvious. The simple truth is this: if you take a shower and dress before doing the bodywork ritual, you are tempted to get on to work and *skip* the self nurturing, spiritually connecting things that open the energy stations and prepare you for quality work and a peaceful day. (You will likely forget the bodywork.) I do almost invariably when I shower and dress first thing in the morning. Life Protocol is done in order for maximum benefit. One thing builds, cleans or stretches for the next.

***

About Makeup: There was a time when I "envied" men's nice skin tone and their lack of the makeup requirement. Gradually I reduced the amount of makeup used, and the quality and color of my skin improved. Commercial makeup (it is changing) is loaded with chemicals that go straight into the blood and impair the body. The "new" mineral powders I believe are better. Just a bit of warmed oil to bring up the circulation, a light swash of mineral powder, a touch of blush powder, some natural looking eye makeup and a lip conditioner such as moringa oil, with mineral based lipstick is all I need. I like to spray my face lightly after all that attention, with a natural rose hydrosol to blend it all. I can easily take or leave any or all of that. My face is much happier now and I don't envy makeup fee men. The plastic bag feeling cover on the skin that restrict energy flow, is gone forever. You will find your own comfortable level of presentation to the public, but I encourage you to be natural and let the beauty of your love be seen uncovered. Even our eyebrows should be left to be. Every one of them is there for a purpose. I love free growing eyebrows that carry out the full expression of the person and reflect light in an unhampered way. The new glamour is *authenticity*. The human face and body are fancy enough without "gilding the lily."

Over-exposure and over-adornment quickly can approach manipulation of others and even idolatry in the Old Testament Biblical sense. Drawing attention to oneself with excessive adornment is a form of idolatry and is a spiritual pitfall. This is an attempt to "self bless"—the pathetic attempt to do what only God can do—bless us beyond the ordinary. When we "self bless" we block the unforeseen blessings that the Universe has for us and that would be ours if we could wait patiently and refrain from trying to take over God's part. "Self blessing" never delivers what we desire.

Many women of today appear to "fix up" so and practice such a deceit with make up and "come-on/go away" tactics that many of our men with high-level integrity are turned off. Authenticity attracts the authentic. The lie has been accepted by many women today that exposure and adornment make them attractive and powerful. To use these methods, attracts and exerts power indiscriminately and does not attract and affect what contributes to their well-being and that of society. To degrade women, is to leave men rather clueless. I challenge women to drop the excess and present themselves honestly to men as their helpers and friends. They will find themselves in love one day, without trying, when the time and person is right. Our men will follow your lead, women—unconsciously of course—and will be easily able to be the men they were designed to be and step out front as progenitors, providers and protectors of the family to forge a New America.

Women will be amazed at the real power they have without deceit, manipulation, or "self blessing"—the power to change the direction of the world by rejecting the lies that are being promoted by those groups and individuals that live and profit in the zone of profanity. Media promotions, sports, and the entertainment business often create wealth and generate influence by glamorizing profanity. In the process women have become degraded. There is a blessed drift, however, in the direction of this new glamour called Authenticity. The popularity of "reality" television shows this new trend. The new American woman has been born. She rejects being degraded in any way. She rejects any attempt to take over the assertive roles of men unless there is none around to do it, and it must be done. She will claim her primary position as one who embraces, receives and nurtures, naturally. She leads the way to our New America. Yang (assertive and aggressive) dominance will give way to Yin (receptive and nurturing) until the energy of Yin in our land becomes too dominant, then the new man will be born who will lead the way again to the Change.

***

About Breakfast Food: The saying: "Eat breakfast like a king, eat lunch like a prince and eat supper like pauper" is a good practice. The body rests, cleanses and rebuilds at night when we sleep. When food is introduced into the body or waiting to be digested, it takes priority and all the other important body functions are put off. Bodywork is best done *before* any heavy eating in the morning. Living with a proper *order* of the day permits the Universe to give us help with the thing that comes next.

Breakfast basics for me are good quality oatmeal with raisins, cinnamon, a bit of maple syrup and organic dairy or coconut milk. A boiled egg with whole grain toast and butter if I am famished. Currently, I like to go out to the garden and cut some greens to simmer with moringa leaf powder (just a teaspoon is enough) and some seasoning with a drizzle of olive oil to have for breakfast with toast and scrambled eggs. I like to add a cup of mango and apricot or some other fruit to my dark blue plate for sweetness and color. My blue plate special! In the refrigerator I keep a container of moringa leaf powder hydrated with filtered water, add fresh ginger and lemon juice. The leaf powder has a large quantity of various nutrients, the ginger compound is potent for immunity and for digestion and the lemon juice adds vitamin C and preserves freshness in the entire cocktail. I drink it for nourishment and refreshment. For my system I find that to slowly simmer the leaf powder and ginger for about five minutes helps make it easier to handle. It is quite potent raw. After simmering about 3 cups of this mixture, I add 3 cups of cold water, juice of half a lemon and 3 or 4 tablespoons of honey. Honey should not be heated much as it changes the compound into something not so good for us.

To warm it to melting temperature is fine. There is a basic rule to *not* give infants heated honey of any kind. When cold water is added to the "cooked" moringa and ginger it becomes barely warm for adding honey. Together with our other holy foods such as coconut, asparagus and avocado, the moringa plant leads the way to better health. My morning "blue plate special" has expanded from the traditional breakfast foods to a wide variety of flavors, colors, textures and nutrients, although I still enjoy bacon, eggs and muffins. Now, however, the bacon is uncured, sweet, chewy, and humanely processed. The eggs are from cage free and organically fed chickens. The bread is whatever I can get that is good. Sometimes we just pray over whatever is before us and eat.

6. Special project work. Finally after our morning rituals, we arrive at the place in the day where we can make some real ripples. Anything can be a special project that is a material expression of the love that we are. It could be something ugly or mean, but we will reserve discussion of that for another book. Our special projects reverberate no matter how small they seem, out to the entire world. In following God's Protocol for your life (His laws and your rules)—your personal opportunities will appear as *coincidences.* In fact, they are coincidences—the moment of "now" where energy lines cross and create an event. This is the birth of destiny beads in your rosary of life—your personal chain of crystalline moments that define who you are, where you are, what you are, what you are doing in life, and with whom.

If you choose not to follow God's Protocol for your life, the quality of your days and nights is determined by the ripple effect of the zone of profanity and by the ripple effect of those who follow Universal laws in the Zone of Holiness. The incoherence of these two meeting is always disturbing. If you are blessed by Grace and intervention (divine anointment) and by your associates, life will be good. You are being prepared for something large in God's purposes and desires. Eventually, God's Protocol will be yours. If not, you will simply be pulled and pushed around by circumstance and cell memory. It may not be horrible, but nowhere near the glorious life you are destined to have by materializing the pattern of love impulses given by your Creator to you at birth.

***

These days, with the internet available, we are almost limitless in the ways we can make a difference and contribute to the quality of life all over and around us. Science partners with Spirit to create the ways to materialize our hearts desires. Each time we find something that clearly chimes with the truth of who we are at our love center (heart), there is science and spirit to help us understand how we can use it to discover our dreams and see them manifest. At this place we gratefully embrace the opportunity and follow our Advocate Voice to act upon it *or not*—it may be our responsibility or that of another. The Advocate will tell you. If it belongs to someone else, let it alone. If you stir someone else's pot, then who will stir yours? We are not responsible to follow every good idea that comes along. The Holy Spirit is our project guide. When we cannot hear the Voice, we simply follow basic Life Protocol an act financially and socially responsible until the Voice is clear.

***

Your Special Project will be clear when the protocol of the morning has been followed. There will be a job—a work of some kind that you—probably only you—can do at this time—the job of immediate importance. Sometimes it is as simple as going to bank and making a deposit or visiting the farmer's market to purchase food for the day. This may be the time to do shopping for someone who is unable to buy for himself. You may need to finish a chapter in your pending book or sign that painting you did the other day. The job is yours alone. It is at the top of the list today. That little rest after breakfast will probably bring the task description forward and you will know what to do. You may be earning a living doing something that takes more time than I have allowed for the Special Project work in the morning. This is a challenge for you to work out—how to earn money for meeting the practical needs of life and at the same time be true to yourself and the natural rhythm and laws of life. I believe it is not only possible, but essential that this Protocol happen for you and for me. Money earned by efforts that contradict natural law that are in place for your well being will not add long run value to your life although it may keep the lights on today. This is your life. Each moment is beautiful, valuable and important. There is plenty of time, but none to waste doing things that contravene your well being. There may be a time when you work in less than ideal conditions and circumstances in your quest for the job that suits your talents and love impulses; but you serve yourself well to treat that job as if it is the best one in the world. Do it without whining and get it done efficiently with commitment to integrity. Everyone and God is watching you in the spiritual sense. Everything you do ripples out to everyone else. Take that job to the next level. Let the one who comes after you to do the same job after you have moved into better circumstances, to have big shoes to fill. Do it with style. *Make it beautiful.* You will find joy and peace in this attitude when you least expect it. Who knows where your work will lead or what person will connect with you because of the way you handle the mundane.

Surprise is one of the best parts of life. The small seeming errands have a rationality that creates the response required to make you do it but the real reason for the job or errand may be apparent only later. Do not underestimate what the Spirit tells you to do. God knows the whole scene. You do not and cannot. Just follow, notice and enjoy what you can. Sometimes a drudge job creeps up to the special project category if time or interest has left a necessary normally unpleasant task undone. So be it. The rewards will come as we work with faith according to our gifts, and as we are led by the Holy Spirit of God. Pray for direction and it will come to you. Know that if you work with God—(you will know by your joy and anticipation of each day)—your own needs and desires will be met and fulfilled beyond your dreams.

No guilt to be had when we get to our special project in the right order of the day. I admit we aren't left with much time after the morning's preparations, yet it is time well spent. So many times we do work for hours out of order that ends up in the trash. This morning "special project time" is gold time. We can proceed at special project time with a slow enjoyment, knowing we have earned the right to do exactly what we are doing and *it is good*. It is our lane and we have a right to be in it! I told myself this out loud as I drove to the Portland, Oregon airport in 1992 as an interstate novice. There were eight lanes to navigate. Don't be embarrassed to talk to yourself. It is a wonderful thing to do, especially if you are a novice at something or it is drudge work. Be a bit careful with this kind of expression in public unless you wear a funny hat.

***

I pick up the work on my special project at the appropriate time of day after morning rituals are over. For me, if I rise at dawn, it is about 10:00 a.m. Special projects are usually jobs that have been on my mind to do that is helpful to my own life or a task that has my name on it that helps someone else. Be sure and don't take on jobs and causes that someone else can do just as well or better. Do only those tasks with your name on it clearly. This takes discernment in your spirit. Say "no" to almost everything. Don't be a doormat for your friends and family or community. My Don't number seven is "don't over-nurture." Each day will hold plenty for you to do with your name planted squarely on it. Limit your time and energy to this project. Work on it for the allotted time in Protocol, then save the remainder of the job for a later date if at all possible—tomorrow. To press your project into lunchtime best be done with awareness and due to apparent *necessity*. The day's Order is something to honor for good reason.

***

At times you will have direction only to wait for God. No projects are special enough for the moment—maybe for the entire day. No highlights appear. This is a receptive rather than an assertive time. Some call it a necessary swing back to the "yin" energy. Accept this time. Do not worry that something is wrong with you. Being comfortable with stillness and quietness is a level of progress. It is a necessary step to becoming someone greater than you have known yourself to be before. It is better than okay to do nothing sometimes. If you feel the absolute need to do something, take a shower, dress comfortably and go outside. Look around and check out the natural world. Soon it will be night and you will be in sync again with the great receptive female type energy. Eventually there is a shift and you can know then what to do again. Enjoy "yin" energy. It is the direction we are headed in this world. Go with that flow. Make your choices with the conscious integrity of an artist or a laboratory scientist. Again, know that one thing builds on or dumps cold water or worse on another. When you follow your Life Protocol you are building on a solid foundation—you day—your life—the future. When it is time to prepare lunch or prepare for lunch, put the special project away neatly. Organize the scatter if your creativity is in scatter mode. I cover my writing piles with navy blue cotton napkins to make order for the next part of my day. "Wash your brushes" and put things away where they belong. Have nothing to distract others, yourself, or trip over. Respect your work and your self. Your work is sacred, as are you.

7. Lunch and Nap: For lunch, I eat fresh fruit and vegetables, good grains and fish, dairy and eggs too, but not much meat. The energy of killed animals is something I don't need in my body. I cannot explain it to sound intelligent but believe it ties me up too much to deal with the ramifications of animal energy in anything but fish, dairy and eggs. When I do eat meat, I offer a special prayer of energy cleansing and thankfulness for the sacrificed life of the animal to my nourishment. Lunchtime and naps go together, as the food you eat affects the quality of your nap and prompts the necessity for it. Our bodies prioritize digesting food. Rest mode is best for this process. Lunch best be simple. There is usually little time to spend fussing around with preparations. My favorite quick food is a midday feast of home grown greens, a few turnips, and a small pone of cornbread baked in my toaster oven in a ceramic bowl. My second favorite lunch is *asparagus soup*, Thai style, with crusty French bread. Recipes follow for your entertainment:

Greens and turnips: Wash greens and turnips, shred greens, cut turnips in quarters, while 1/4 cup chopped onion is slowly sizzling with olive or coconut oil in a *non-aluminum* pot on the stove. You can use garlic (or whatever you like) too if you wish. Mustard greens and collards love garlic. Toss in the greens and turnips with a little water and cover to cook slowly about 15 minutes.

Cornbread: In a ceramic baking dish...I like the larger ramekins...a small iron skillet works too...place 3 tablespoons of coconut or olive oil or a combo of both. Add chopped or sliced onion to the dish with oil and place it in the cold oven turned on to 375 degrees. While the oil and onion heats, mix the cornbread: In a medium small bowl mix together with wire whisk: 3/4 cup corn meal, 1/4 cup flour, 1/4 teaspoon sea salt, pinch of baking soda, and 1/2 teaspoon sugar. Into the dry mixture, pour a scant cup of buttermilk, mix with a rubber scraper/spatula in folding motion until milk absorbed, then bring out the heated oil and onions and add them lightly with a rubber scraper in folding motion, to the cornbread batter. Place a piece of parchment paper you have cut to fit, in the bottom of the baking dish, wiping sides of dish with oil using the parchment and placing the parchment on the bottom, oiled side up. Pour in the batter and bake the cornbread for about 25 minutes until golden brown. Take the bread out of the oven and place it on a wire rack. Run a knife around the sides of the baking dish, then tump it out onto a plate, removing the parchment. Serve with real butter.

Asparagus soup: In a blender, mix a can of asparagus tips or cooked fresh asparagus, 1/3 cup coconut milk powder, dash of salt, dash of pepper to taste (canned asparagus will have salt added usually), 1 teaspoon curry powder, 1/4 teaspoon red curry paste and a cup of warm water. Place the lightly pureed mixture in a small heavy steel pot and heat to desired temperature. You may want to thin this with more water. If you want to take it up a level, garnish the soup with a few lightly steamed asparagus tips. Crusty bread is good with a spread of garlic butter heated on low in your toaster oven until just right. Leave the dishes in organized chaos at or in the sink, put on your nap suit, and crawl into bed with no guilt.

8. The Sacred Nap: This is my favorite time of day. I have Universal permission, even a mandate, to observe a guilt free rest to re-adjust my priorities and my energy. This means ten finger meditation (to be discussed later here), prayer, and self Acupressure while simply listening for a Word from the Spirit. I most often use the light touch, dual point method with tone singing (acoustical resonance therapy to be discussed later) as a catalyst for releasing stuck energy (stress). I stay down an hour or more by the clock. Sometimes I sleep. I command myself to rest an hour. If I want to get up four minutes sooner, I say "no" to myself. Often that last four minutes is the most beneficial. God has a way of blessing obedience. It was the Spirit that gave me the one-hour rule. Your nap timing may be different. After waking with the dawn, reading, writing, praying, adjusting energy, bodywork, shower, dressing, special projects and lunch, what right minded person would feel it necessary to keep on going without stopping for rest? If your work will not permit this personal care, find another job. The entire world would change for good, if everyone took a nap after a healthy lunch. I like to eat lunch at home so that I can change into my "nap suit" and flop into bed instantly after I lay my fork down. Any delay causes me tension. The nap suit I wear is light cotton pajama pants and a many-times-washed white T shirt with a stretched and scalloped neck line—pure comfort and my ideal costume for resting. If you try this you will notice the different quality energy settling down for a nap in day clothes from when you settle to rest in your nap suit. Honoring the nap and the nap suit, gives me the feeling of two days in one. The quality of afternoon and night is raised.

9. Tea Time: This is usually about 3:00 p.m. and amounts to simply sitting for a few minutes to recapture the sense of myself. Sometimes I eat a cookie or two with the tea. I've been known to have coffee sometimes at 3:00 p.m. although I feel better about tea without sugar. My coffee has rich cream and sugar and is brewed in an espresso machine...powerful...therefore once in the morning is ideally my limit. I like coffee that is organic from sources that pay the producers a fair price. This is money well spent. In the hot summertime of Louisiana, the blended drink with blueberries, vinegar, ice, water and honey with a handful of fresh basil give me just the energy lift I need. I call it my "blueberry abstention" because it has the kick and zip of a margarita without the interference. One of my favorite hot teas in winter or whenever I want it, is simply a few slices of fresh ginger in hot water with lemon juice with a teaspoon of maple syrup. The health benefits are great and the pleasure is equal. As I enjoy my tea time treat, I allow myself to just be—sometimes to watch

Nature's doings sounds and smells. One of these drinks and a cookie gives me all the nourishment I need for the afternoon drudge work and play. During tea time I have permission from the Universe to just sit with a relatively vacant mind for awhile. Your work is well served by observing this special time of day. It is a holy time.

10. Drudge Work and Happy Hour: Drudge work assignments come in for duty about 3:30 p.m. This is the time of day to do things I tend to put off like paying bills. I clean something needy, put away clothes, make necessary purchases or do errands. This is the time of day to do things engaging the left, rational, part of the brain. Sometimes I talk to my self to insure the use of my left brain, with words such as: "You must do this, Baby (spoon full of sugar makes the medicine go down). Once you get started it will be fine. You can do it. It will be done right. Let's get going now, no more delay. No one else can do this job like you can." I force myself to do "adult", rational, mundane things at this time of day. When I skimp on the drudge work, it eventually rises to the level of "urgent" and requires attention at special project time. Then my special project time is cheated. You see how that goes. Sometimes a large "special project" becomes necessary to do at drudge time. There is Grace, but daily order and honoring Protocol is essential to the quality of life. We cannot do everything our rational brain says needs to be done, all at once. I work with drudgery beginning about 3:30 p.m. for an hour, then go to the next item of Protocol leaving anything undone until later. Spending too much time in the drudge is not usually necessary. What is really important gets done. Unless it is truly an urgency such as a bank deposit is required immediately, someone may step on something gross, slip, or the smell is bad—it should be worked into daily Protocol without cheating other part of the day to get drudge work done. If our bodywork is left off and the personal energy is stuck, good work in the drudge or special project time slot is most difficult. Even drudge work should flow and be almost, if not really, fun. When drudge work follows the ideal order of the day, it is fun, satisfying and helps the people we live with tremendously. Drudge work done in order sets the stage nicely for the next scene of life. After the "drudge" there is usually some slack time for play. I go outside and look around, visit with a friend or family person. Sometimes I work on some art. "Play" is a large category and the personal preference is yours.

***

Five days a week we do our drudge work but on Saturday we play, doing whatever we want to. Sunday is a day of rest. No drudge work required or recommended. On Sunday we are to lay back, feel what we are about and let our spirits expand beyond the usual. Going to church, when we have found a group of kindred spirits, is a fine thing to do on Sunday. When we can be with family too, what a blessing Sundays can be.

About Happy Hour: If you are blessed enough to have some time between drudge work and supper it is "happy hour" around the world. I enjoy a special drink with someone I like to be with. The blueberry abstention described hereinabove is great—fresh or frozen blueberries, ice, water, vinegar and honey. I also enjoy lemon juice, maple syrup, fresh basil, together with ice and water. Alcohol is a downer (not happy) for me. These perky fruit coolers activate the body's night time rituals of restoration and prepare you to feel good the next day.

11. Prepare Your Food and Eat Before 7:00 p.m. then Play: The two items, supper and playtime—are linked together because to play easily we eat less. Supper is shared with my family sometimes and other times I just snack on whatever I want or need to round out the day's intake of fuel. It's best to leave off carbohydrates at night and pick up some extra greens and protein. The greens with their fiber, calcium and magnesium help the digestive system reorganize during the night and protein builds and repairs. The carbs turn into energy which we don't need during sleep. At night, the body completes the digestive process, renews and repairs for the next day. If I get really hungry *after seven p.m.*, my choice is a peeled apple or an unpeeled apple. I slip up occasionally and eat a piece of cheesecake at midnight. I am a work in progress just like you. To feel "full" in the morning is a bummer. I love the clean empty feeling of a fine tuned digestive system upon awakening.

After supper, our energy changes gears. It's time for more play. After supper playtime is a space of energy during the day to do whatever we want to, even to recapitulate—take stock and summarize. A big glass of water goes well at this time to hydrate for the night. Play is anything I want to do, where I want to do it and with whom, or alone. No reasons needed or any thought of productivity. It lasts till sundown. At sundown it is time to make Order around me in my personal and home space. I clean the kitchen if I have the strength, or not, look around and check for things out of Order. I am not an obsessive housekeeper, but I know instinctively when things are in or out of order at this time of day. Tomorrow is new with new assignments and new energy. I don't want any old energy to be in my way of the potentials in tomorrow's beginning. When you become a Protocol Chief with practice, *it's all play time* even the drudge work and making Order at the end of the day.

I take a bath or shower at night. Three showers a day is not unusual for me. I enjoy the feeling of fresh clean energy. During the day we all exude substances that contain old energy and toxins. To begin the night with clean skin is a health promoting practice at the least. Toxins (substances the body lets go of that it does not want) are re-absorbed at night if not bathed away. Sensitive noses can detect these toxins. It is good Protocol at night, to shower or bathe before sleep even if it is nothing but a rinse off—including the head. Since the nighttime is prime for our bodies to clean and repair we need to help. The extra blessing is a better sleep when we feel clean and fresh. If we sleep *with* someone, a bath is the caring and smart thing to do.

At bedtime, when I feel inclined to same, I read energy work books and practice the Seven Doors, thinking of how they affect me and others. I practice on myself and feel blessed to have these tools available to manage my own energy flow. I drink some water, raise the windows and shades, watch the night scene shadow and take in the evening air, thanking God and praying for all that comes up, then releasing it in every detail to God, knowing my job for the night is to rest.

12. Sleep: I sleep my eight or more hours after the sun goes down and it is dark outside. This is natural and is harmonious with the body's circadian rhythm (designed-in order). Sometimes, however, life is so exciting that I stay up until midnight. Sleep is sacred. It "knits up the raveled sleeve of care" said Will Shakespeare. To know the basics of Acupressure or "energy adjustment" is a valuable skill to use for yourself at night when your energy is out of balance or when you have discomfort. There are classes available in various places all over the world. Anyone can learn. It is simple to hold your right finger pads on one point on the body lightly and your left finger pads on another to release stuck energy. To sing a sound at the same time gently sets up vibrations in the body and gives Acupressure or holding a special power. In Jinshindo° Acupressure we are taught to use gentle but firm pressure. In TKM° energy balancing we are taught to use only light touch. I use gentle but firm pressure to make contact with the energy stations, then back off and hold with light touch while I sing the sounds as a catalyst to effect the release of resistance. Using sound is for self help. As mentioned in the following Chapter devoted to energy release, I don't sing when working on another. My good friend Donna, who is certified in many healing arts, and who has perception beyond the ordinary, says that using the voice to consciously make sounds, especially the sounds of our energy "chakras," is the only way to "massage the brain."

By dusk, the energy is changing from yang to yin—becoming calmer. Calm activities are in order. I turn off all the overhead lights in the house after sundown. I am very sensitive to sound and light and want no stimulating music or light after sundown. "Night life" is for the birds where I am concerned. Even the birds know to fold their wings and speak softly to each other at night. The wisdom of "early to bed, early to rise" is not just for old folks, children and farmers. The early morning when we rise has much to offer the body, mind and soul of human beings. The natural peace of early evening is the time to get clean, put on the most comfortable clothing possible, get in bed, listen and watch God present his bird and bug concert, the pre-night (dusk) display of color in the skies, the His dramatic shadow show. What entertainment! It is delicious to have a couple of hours after supper to read the subject of my service, dream, be thankful and meditate.

Part B: Lagniappe (a bonus)

About the Night: Everything is simplified by lovely darkness when there is peace. Peace is one of the gifts rewarding the Protocol described here. There are certainly times when we feel bad and sad even with the best laws and the most faithful following of the same. In a later Chapter here, I relate to you what I know about what to do then.

On a peaceful night, the sauna is a major treat for body and soul. The ideal sauna is an outdoor wood fired sauna like the Indian sweat lodge and the Russian bania. In this ideal scene the group sits together free of clothing and sweats with plant scented steam; then afterwards in the heat, they tap each other vigorously with branches of soft leaves and supple stems to bring up the toxins and released them. Spiritually, I suspect that cell memories can be healed to some extent by this process, particularly if the person being flogged is spiritually attuned to God by whatever name He is known. After the steamy sauna and branch tapping, the skin is pink then the bather takes a cold shower or rolls in the snow a bit. My Russian neighbor, Marina, tells me about her experience with the bania in her homeland and how it equalizes everyone. Where she lived in Russia, the ladies bathed together and separately, the men bathe together. While on Lasqueti Island, the whole island (men and women) took an outside, wood fired sauna together on Wednesday nights and on Sunday nights, then took a cold shower outside of the sauna. Nicholas and I opted out. I had my reasons. Son Nick simply wasn't ready for the experience. Everything good happens in its own time. An infrared sauna is located inside my home and is electrically powered. The infrared energy of the sun is duplicated and goes deep into the cells to stimulate the release of toxins. It is ready to use in 6 minutes after turning it on. It is made of wood and sits in our guest/sewing room quite nicely. It has a window and a glass door with a curtain on the outside. The bench inside would seat two people easily but my sauna-ing is done alone for 30 minutes at 130 F degrees. After a post sauna shower, I drink some water, raise windows and shades, watch the night scene and shadow and take in the evening air, thanking God and praying for all that comes up, then release it in every detail to God, knowing my job for the night is to sleep. I am invited by the Universal rhythm to retire to my sleeping chambers at sundown. Rarely do I sleep at that time, but I have the right to do so, because of our earthly circadian rhythm. No guilt for going to bed early—it's natural. Before the electric lights, there was little else to do after sundown. When people around me say "What? It's only 6:30 and you're going to bed?!" I laugh, knowing it's certainly fine to sleep at sundown if I am really tired. A rule I try to keep at night is "no thinking after 8:00 p.m."

Thinking is not feeling and is not who we are. It is simply a tool that helps us manage our feelings and desires. Over thinking deprives a person of the moment's opportunities. Not only are we obliged to deny the impulsive habit of wandering thought in our spare time, we are best served to avoid it. We, the crown of creation, have been given this tool to use when it is necessary, to help us make decisions for appropriate action. It is a tool to provide detachment and to be used for evaluation but is not a substitute for faith, spiritual pondering, or creative imagination.

Thought, or use of the intellect (it bears the energy color yellow) tends to produce guilt and more confusion than truth if used too much. It creates an illusion of reality. Thinking cancels authentic experience when fear energy searches for a way to block the moment's event. Thinking something does not make it so or not so. God makes it so or not so. Thinking is an intellectual tool we often employ when we have time on our hands, especially when we have trouble falling asleep. Thought is often taken over by the Adversary. If you must think do it before 8:00 p.m. After 8:00 p.m. the stage is set for thankfulness and prayer, not *thinkfull-ness* and fear. After 8:00 p.m. it is time to prepared for bed and sleep—a soothing bath, some herbal tea, stretches, some self Acupressure to release energy blocks—to restore basic order to your personal self and space. If you are blessed with a revelation from God that encourages thought, write it down quickly in some poetic or coded form for remembrance the next day. Don't worry a bit about rationality. The next morning you will know more about what it means to your everyday life and Assignment of Responsibility. Working out a practical way (before 8:00 p.m.) to accomplish a task assigned to you by the Holy Spirit, is legitimate thought within the confines of integrity and prudence. This is why we were given the gift of thought. To use it for worry, fear, or regret is abusing a God given trust. To think at the wrong time creates a false sense of reality and produces unhealthy chemicals in the body. It feels unpleasant. This body reaction helps us recognize lies and reject them. The more sensitive we become to this unpleasant feeling in the presence of lies the more quickly we can toss out the false before it distorts our energy pattern and causes stress or worse, a life style aberration. Anything presented to the spirit that is deceptive, immediately creates waste chemicals for the body to eliminate as quickly and effectively as possible.

Even the use of imagination to consider possible pleasant situations and states of being can be carried too far and result in unpleasant physical energy. The moment's truth and the magic of coincidence designed by God especially for your nourishment, enlightenment, and delight is a superior experience to the pressing of thoughts and the entertainment of fantasies. Imagination is not useful when we live in the Zone of Holiness. We don't need it. We miss God's blessings by being too busy with our own attempts to "self bless." Thinking is having a conversation with oneself in the mind. I often do plenty of thinking after 8:00 p.m. but there is a kind voice from somewhere telling me to hush. I am invited not to think after 8:00 p.m. The message I sense is God is saying: "Look here child, go to sleep, I do not usually talk to people after 8:00 p.m. unless it is in a dream. The evil one, however, will talk to you. Robbing you of sleep is fun for Satan. Whatever problems you think you have worked out at night will be yet to reconsider the next morning. You will likely want to junk your night time solutions."

About Night Work: I like the "no work after 7:00 p.m." law. Unless it is a major project with a firm date of completion, "no work after 7:00" is best observed. If I don't start letting go of thought at 7:00 p.m. by the time I am ready to sleep, my mind remains in high gear. A busy, alert mind will hold you at attention until the wee hours. "No work after 7:00 p.m." is a Universal law that we best observe. In days past, before electricity and computers and the like, no one worked because it was usually dark and candlelight was ineffective. So often work products after 7:00 p.m. are no good anyway and the time was basically wasted.

When You Wake Up in the Night: I have learned something important lately. When I wake up in the night, it's most often about *water*... releasing water and taking it in. The "necessary room" is a blessing to have nearby. I drink all the water I have the patience to take in when I awaken at night. The clear message is that my body needs water to help with the cleansing and repair process going on at that specific time of night.

About Food: To maintain strength, balance, and purity in the body and mind, we are well served to select food that is close to how it was grown—fresh, whole, organically produced (no chemicals or pesticides—and stay away from the lesser items. Some things that pose as food are tricky as they fool the eye and taste buds and tempt us with artificial taste enhancers, color and flavor. These artificial colors and flavors are neurotoxins. Once you begin to feed yourself natural, lovingly prepared fresh food daily, and avoid the other, your body will not want anything less. It will speak to you in all kinds of ways and say "where has this been all my life—the jig's up—no more of that bad stuff—it's over." Magic happens when you treat the body right. You'll see if you haven't seen already. The Creator rewards those who follow the universal laws of health. If you can't follow the laws and rhythms of nature, and take care of your body in the work you are doing, find something else to do. To sacrifice health for work is not smart or rewarding in the long run. Basically, it is dumb. I know because I have done it in the past.

About Water: The first "rule of body" that my Advocate, the Holy Spirit, tells me is to "first find water." With enough water that contains health supporting minerals, we have a major part of the nourishment we need. I brought several gallons of filtered water from West Monroe with me for my ten days in Hemet,

California where I studied Jinshindo° Acupressure. The desert and hot springs are about an hour away, so I thought I was going to the desert. Actually A Ranch is in foothills of the San Jacinto Mountains. To my great delight, A Ranch has the best well water I have ever tasted. When I left, I took a couple of gallons of it with me to drink on the trip back to Louisiana. The teaching ranch is small but the infrastructure is fine. The Acupressure students were advised to follow drought rules to conserve water. Too many people using too much water can create an overdraft on this precious resource. This is a truth for all the world.

Try to find drinking water that contains all the good minerals such as calcium, magnesium, sodium and potassium—the big four—without the toxins like lead and chlorine. Deep, deep well water is usually great. If you have the money, dig a well for your home. Test the water to be sure it is not contaminated and find out what the mineral content is. The plastic containers used for bottled water, even good spring water, contaminate the drink unless they are especially made to be non-leaching. Water contains so many of the nutrients we need to be healthy. Proper hydration is probably the most important physical need we have in the world today. It solves many health issues and prevents more. Finding good drinking water best be a priority. While attending the Acupressure workshop in California in 2007 some of the students were visiting in the kitchen and dining area as we did for every meal and at our break times. We were talking about our dreams. One of the students mentioned how he was looking for a place to build a home. I mentioned to him that I was also searching for location with a pure, highly nourishing water source. He looked directly at me with an "I know the answer" look and told me about a place in his homeland where the water was perfect. I didn't forget and want to visit that place someday soon. I keep some things secret to protect the privacy of my friends and associates. The Spirit has always told me in the quiet, persistent way of the Advocate: *"first find water."*

About Air: If the air is polluted where you live. *Move.* If you think you can't move, then buy a good air purifier. Ventilate your home if the air outside is decent. Even it is not perfect, open windows and ventilate. Fumes build up from things inside our homes that are not health promoting. Try to live in a place where the air is *wonderful.* It will make your feel like and act like a nicer person. Why not, given the importance of breath and breathing for the well being of your body, mind and soul and for those who follow you in life.

About Probiotics: The cultured milk probiotic called "kefir" is a powerful, creamy drink when you want something to "eat up" the extra sugar in your digestive system and discourage the unwelcome visitors who try to live with you, such as yeast and parasites. There are web stores such as wildernessfamilynaturals. com that sell starter granules that are a great to keep in the refrigerator to make your own kefir. Kefir is a yogurt like milk drink that contains certain pro-biotics (friendly bacteria) that are said to colonize in the intestines and help maintain the delicate ecosystem for processing our food. If you make your own kefir, you can remake it easily by saving a spoonful in your glass or container, add some milk and let it sit out overnight. The starter spoonful will feed on the sugar in the milk and create a brand new batch of pro-biotic to drink the next day. This is probably the cheapest health boon available to take inside your body.

The Russians people have long sustained and maintained themselves on the cultured milk kefir, beet soup and their outdoor sauna bath called the "bania." The popular health modality of "tapping" I suspect has the same roots as the Russian bania and the Indian sweat lodge where it was the common practice to "flog" each other briskly with supple leafy branches to stir the chi (vital personal energy) and a dredge up the toxins to release by sweating. No more physically vibrant people exist than Russian men and women and the Native American Indians whose ancestors practiced this steam bath and stimulation on the surface of the skin. In Russia, rolling in the snow was the finale, closing pores and contributing to the over-all cleansing of mind, body and soul. I suspect this all was an attempt to cleans unnecessary and/or impairing cell memory. I use the indoor infrared sauna, but intend someday to have something more akin to the sweat lodge and bania, outside. Marina can barely wait.

About Alcohol: Taking inside your body anything known to be toxic is not wise if your purpose is to love and nurture yourself in order to love and nurture others and be all the person you can be. This includes alcohol and any kind of drug preparation—both causing acidity in the body which de-mineralizes the bones by drawing minerals out of them to create a balanced acid/alkaline level—necessary for optimal function.

Choices based on your highest values made at difficult times, without compromise, builds a quality of life that reveals your true identity, the desires of your deepest heart, and forms a structure that will allow you to peacefully enjoy your days and nights without guilt and fear. Those around you will be taught by your example and inspired.

In the summertime, I enjoy a potent blender mix of peeled fresh cucumber added to fruit such as banana with orange juice and ice. To get the tang and zip (energy shift) of a "happy hour" drink without alcohol, I make my "blueberry abstention" described loosely above and reiterated here because of its vitality: frozen raw blueberries, a teaspoon of apple cider vinegar, a cup of ice, 2 tablespoons of raw honey and a little filtered water blended into a smooth drink—add a sprig of fresh basil and you have something much better than any alcoholic drink. You actually have a delicious, spirit lifting, health cocktail. Alcohol is disturbing to my personal energy pattern therefore I abstain. It opens the door to the energy of profanity. Enough of an alcoholic drink consumed to the point one feels a change, interferes with the personal energy pattern. When personal energy is interfered with or incoherent, he can easily slip into the state of forgetting who he is at the crossroads of choice. The forgetting can lead to actions one may regret and that ripple out to affect others—people you have not yet met, including future children. King Solomon of Bible times, sums it up nicely:

"Who hath woe? Who hath sorrow? Who hath contentions? Who hath babbling? Who hath wounds without cause? Who hath redness of eyes? They that tarry long at the wine; they that go to seek mixed wines. Look not thou upon the wine when it is red, when it giveth his colour in the cup, when it moveth itself aright. At the last it biteth like an adder. Thine eyes shall behold strange women, and thine heart shall utter perverse things...."
—King Solomon, *The Bible*, Proverbs 23:29-33

When considering the creation of a family—future generations—there is a new book on the subject of preparing to conceive, birth and parent a child and appears to be the only book of its kind yet to be published. It is written by Glenn T.

King, originator of the powerful TKM° energy therapy modality and is entitled *Wonderfully Made*. This book contains essential wisdom of life that we all need, points the way to a new awareness of changes we can make in our daily life that vitally impact our children and theirs. It is a harbinger and guide for the New American.

***

Energy flow adjusting is an essential part of my Daily Do(s). The next chapter explores in some depth, our God given power to lay hands on the body and cause stuck energy to move and flow, making way for a higher state of well being to take place. We are designed to self-repair. Using the hands to touch two, different, but associated energy "stations" in the body simultaneously, releases energy blocks in one's own body or another and it is safe and easy. The following chapter provides clues and directions for giving personal energy the freedom to flow when it feels restricted or "stuck." To show loving care for yourself by memorizing and using the energy releases in the next chapter daily, prepares you to receive divine blessings of the Universe. When blessings are in order, we best be prepared or risk denying ourselves the right to receive them. So many blessings are passed up by not being ready. Part of being ready is to have a positive state of mind, patiently expecting God's unsurpassable gifts.

The seven energy releases described next are pleasant and effective ways to bridge the gap between you and the next blessing. They give our hands something to do while we wait and enter a peaceful, receptive state of mind.

The routines I describe here are those I use daily to help myself release stuck energy. It is part of my basic daily protocol. Sometimes I use only the first one or two of the others although working through all seven like a dance is best. With practice, you will know what to use and when, for your best flow. Beginning with the Yellow Door, the solar plexus relaxes and promotes tension release in the other stations. The releases I have composed are similar to the sequences available in Jinshindo® Acupressure and the sequences of TKM® but not the same. They are dual station, light touch remedies for helping your body repair and maintain a feeling of well-being.

I use the catalyst of vocal sound in these self-help sequences for quick release of stuck energy. Vocal tone sound is not used with TKM® energy flow modality, nor have I encountered any use of singing during Jinshindo® Acupressure sessions or classes. Using voice is tricky as it can cause stress in some people, which cancels its value. Do not sing if it is uncomfortable for you. Singing in the "holy zone" increases focus with a peculiar vibrational power to dissolve resistance. Your voice—your vibrations—your stuck energy releases. The Voice chapter here explores the feeling and mechanics for "holy zone" song.

I have arrived at the specific examples called "Doors" to freedom through prayer, research, experimentation and revelation. My intention has been to simplify. If they are simple yet effective, more people can be helped. Although not intended to be anatomically precise, some drawings are included as maps to help you visualize where to place your hands to accomplish the location release.

5

The Seven Doors to Energy Freedom

The following Seven Doors are designed to open and free the main "energy stations" of the body. They have been condensed into their simplest form to permit immediate access to the power of helping yourself decongest energy blocks with your own hands. They are symbolic Doors to help the energy flow necessary to materialize the unique self that you are. The Doors are especially pleasant to use if you memorize them. They are coherent with the seven energy centers called "chakras," together with related color and vocal sound—powerful influences beyond imagination.

Energy flow can be restored and maintained in various other ways. What works for one person is sometimes different from what is effective for another. With experimentation, prayer, research and revelation you will find the ways that serves you best. When the mind is open to new ideas, even a bit, the use of this ancient system of dual touch stations can create a dramatic difference in the way our days go and flow. The hands on self help described here is safe, loving, and always available. It is a health supporting modality that empowers the person using it. We best organize our lives in a way that avoids dependence on others when possible. The Doors can be used to quiet the mind and calm the body while waiting on the Universe to bless.

Go through these Doors dressed in loose, comfortable cotton clothing. Synthetic materials bind the flow of energy. Leave off the wristwatch, metal rings, jewelry, and keep the electronic gadgets at least ten feet away. Daily practice of the following described releases helps to relieve physical and e-motional (energy frequency quality and velocity) troubles. If this hands on help does not relieve the problem, and there are some problems people suffer that are outside the scope of this energy decongesting Chapter, the meditative state that you enjoy while practicing the Doors moves you into sync with Universal wisdom. In this state of peace and enlightenment, you are most apt to understand what you are to do to go further with solving your problems, whatever they are. Eliminating fear is a major help to finding the healing and help we desire.

To begin, prop yourself up with pillows—one under the knees with knees touching. You can sit up in bed or in a recliner. If you lie down, rather than sit up, do not sing, just make the sound mentally. To sing lying down creates tension because it is unnatural. If singing becomes stressful, difficult, or uncomfortable, do not sing, simply make the sound mentally or leave it off. The absence of stress while going through the Doors is more important than making the Door sounds. Finding a comfortable place and enough pillows is the first step. I use the abbreviations LH for "left hand", RH for "right hand" and fps for "finger pads." The drawings show a person without clothing to facilitate station location. Do not demand perfection of yourself. Your intention to create the feeling and state of well-being, and your enjoyment of this process is primary.

THE YELLOW DOOR

The color "yellow" has an energy frequency that correlates with the energy frequency of the solar plexus (midsection of body just below ribs). The sound "aw" as in "now" has an energy frequency that correlates with the solar plexus and color "yellow." Having the ability to relax tension in this particular area and permit a free flow of energy is a valuable skill for maintaining health and materializing your love. You are releasing stuck energy at the body's "Grand Central Station."

Step One: Place RH-fps (right hand finger pads) or palm on crown of head and simultaneously place LH-fps (left hand finger pads) on left sit bone.

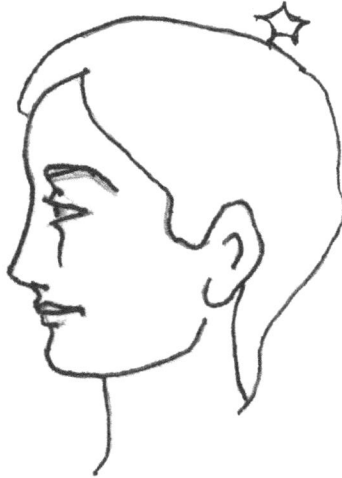

Figure 1: Crown of Head

Figure 2: Sit Bone

Step Two: Quietly sing the sound "now"—focusing the tone at your right nose bone (bone not cartilage), temporarily forgetting that you have a throat, tongue and jaw for now, and connecting the nose focus with a focus just below the navel in the abdomen. This is the recipe for making a holy (free and open) sound. Some people do this automatically and others, like myself, have to work at it to make it happen. The nose point correlates with the mind; the abdominal point correlates with the body. Later, when this sounds become open and free you can add soul—the color, expression, and diction that you desire, with your jaw, lips and tongue. Chapter Ten here explores voice as a catalystic frontier. If you had rather not sing, simply think the sound "now."

Hold this posture for a minute or two while singing or thinking "now" or until you notice a shift in energy towards relaxation in the solar plexus area. Without singing, the release may take longer. Always breathe normally—no pushing. You never have to "take" a breath—it happens automatically after you let it out in singing. Simply accept the breath with gratitude. You have all the air you need.

Repeat on other side with opposite hands.

When singing in the "holy zone" you may engage small muscles that you have almost never used. Take care to breathe normally and naturally. To breathe in such a way that the rhythm is erratic, pushed, held too long or gasped makes tension in the throat and jaw area and everywhere else.

The vocal experience may be a little scary at first, but it is powerful. Remember to sit up when you sing. This use of sound vibration works as a catalyst to speed up the release. If your voice breaks or sounds weird, that means you are trying something new and there is some tension to relax somewhere. "

At some point after a minute or so, you usually feel a shift that can be described as energy from the inside gently pushing your hands away. When you find yourself taking a deep breath prompted by something you haven't controlled, you are free to move on. A ticklish feeling in the ribs and abdomen is a sign of great progress! You are entering a vocal "holy zone."

As you practice these Seven Doors, you will become more and more aware of the energy quality and flow in your body. You cannot always control what your energy does, nevertheless, you can learn to work with it for well being. When stuck energy moves, we flow! When we flow we can bless others. The free solar plexus gives courage to the heart to love.

The Green Door of the heart now beckons to be opened.

THE GREEN DOOR

The heart energy color is "green" and the sound frequency is "ah" as in "yaah" and "naah." We are wise to listen to the heart and respond to its advice. To say "naah" when pushed to do or think something unauthorized by the heart, demonstrates self-respect and love. When we were two years old it was no problem to say "naah." Then came the pressures of others and the pressures of society telling us that the *yes* response to their demands was better. We lose our sense of self when we give in to these pressures. There comes a time in the evolvement of each person when saying "naah" is not only permitted, it is essential. To restore the misshapen and devalued in our lives, we have the privilege and grace now to say "naah!"

Looking at someone and seeing the real person helps him have the courage to heal. To be able to see or sense another's love pattern (his heart) and look through and past the trappings, attitudes, beliefs and physical results of bad choices—is a gift of healing. We are called to look beyond the fault to the need in others. To contact our own original love pattern and believe it can be cleansed of old, offending cell memory and return to contact with the holiness and purity of our original impulses, is the beginning of our own healing in every part of life. Don't be offended when others say "naah" and don't worry about offending others when your heart says "naah" and your voice follows.

There are many touch/holding sequences to revitalize the heart energy in the energy flow modalities of Jinshindo˚ and in TKM˚—all good and powerful. I have drawn inspiration from both and deliver to you three that are simple to use by almost anyone. This next release can be done on yourself or another person. The key is to find the fifth thoracic vertebra. Count down the spine from the first large vertebra at the base of my neck, using it as number one. On myself, the fifth thoracic vertebra happens to be down as far as I can reach.

Step One: Place the RH-fps (right hand middle finger along with its companions) on your T-5 (fifth thoracic) vertebra. Gently hold it while looping your left thumb over and touching your left little fingernail. If you are working on someone else, embrace their left little finger with your left hand while holding your right hand on their T-5 vertebra. When working on yourself, hold these areas and sing a soft sound of "yaah" or "naah" focusing on the right side of the nose bone and the abdomen, forgetting the throat, jaw and tongue.

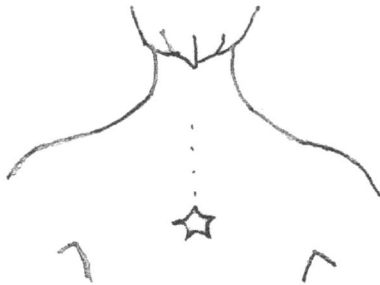

Figure 3: Fifth Thoracic Vertebra

Figure 4: Looping Thumb Pads Over Ring Fingernail

Although it is optional, the sound made in the resonant "holy zone," no matter how quietly or how shakily, will immediately unlock tension and radiate vibrations to the heart area, helping to release stuck energy and create the kind of flow that supports the expression of love. Hold these two areas simultaneously for a few breaths, until you feel a subtle, light expansion of energy in the mid back area towards relaxation. Hold as long as you desire. A deep effortless breath is often prompted with the release.

Step Two: While continuing to hold/touch the T-5 vertebra with your right hand, take your left finger pads to the area on the sole of your left foot located in the middle under the big toe. Hold/touch and sing or think the sound until the pleasant shift occurs.

Figure 5: Middle Inside of Foot

This release is done only with the left side energy stations complementing the fifth thoracic vertebra (T-5) touch/hold. There is no "other side" experience. It is complete with T-5, plus the Left little fingernail and the middle inside of foot sole.

I have included here two more heart energy releases that make this section longer than I wanted but are so helpful for breast, heart and lungs that I was compelled to give them to you. They are called "Triune I" and "Triune II." The word "triune" came at first thought to be their names because three energy stations are contacted at once to generate the energy flow.

TRIUNE I

The description provided here applies to both sides. Of course use opposite hands for the "other" side experience. It is always best to do the Triune releases on both sides where possible for balance. Remember to recline on a bed or chair with knees together, propped up with a pillow for maximum comfort and effect.

Step One: Place left thumb knuckle against the tense (usually) place at the base of the front left side neck just above the collarbone, pressing gently against the muscle, and with the left remaining finger pads hold the tense (usually) neck muscles on the left side of spine. Feel for the tension. It may be all down the neck to the base and even into the shoulder area. When one place releases, ease to the next.

Figure 6: Top of Collarbone

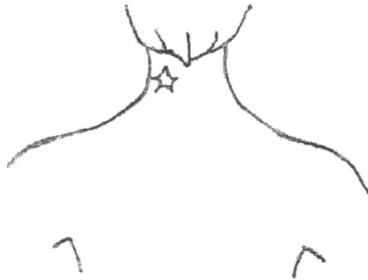

Figure 7: Side of Back Neck

Step Two: Simultaneously, while continuing the hold the previous energy stations, place the finger pads of your right hand on the area at the back arm/shoulder joint, at the upper and outermost part of the joint. Move the right hand under the left arm to reach this shoulder area.

Press to contact, then release to a very light touch after the tension begins to loosen. This release is immediately accelerated by quietly singing a tone in the holy zone such as "yaah" or "naah" for a few minutes or until you feel the shift towards relaxation. Of course sing whatever tone you desire. Focusing at the right nose bone and the abdominal area is the primary objective, which releases the throat, jaw and tongue tension. The vibrations instantly move through the body and head if you can do this.

Figure 8: Back Arm/Shoulder Joint

TRIUNE II

This release helps restore energy flow in the upper back, breast, chest, and rib area.

Step One: Place left thumb under the left arm area on the first rib in between space you can get to comfortably on the left side of the chest. The left finger pads will land on the breast/chest area.

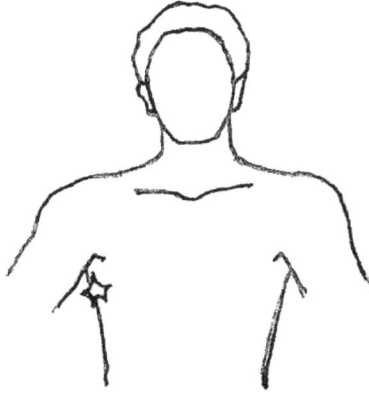

Figure 9: Rib Space Under Arm

Hold these two energy stations gently while the right hand palm or fingers gently holds the center of the chest in whatever way is comfortable.

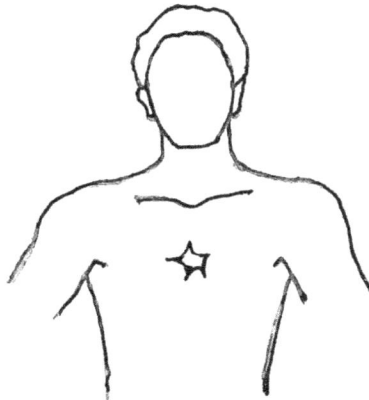

Figure 10: Center of Chest

Keep this touch/hold going for a few minutes until you are prompted to take a deep breath or until you notice a shift in energy towards relaxation.

Step Two: Keep your right hand on the center of the chest. Simultaneously, beginning at the front arm/shoulder joint on the pectoral muscle, use your LH-fps to touch/hold gently down the side of the ribs around to the rib space under the arm by touching the spaces in between ribs and holding for a minute or so.

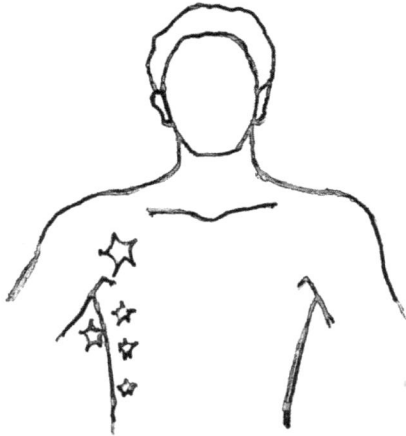

Figure 11: Stations Between Ribs

This is a powerful release for stuck energy in the lungs, heart, breast and other vital areas of the body, as you will notice as you experiment with this sequence. Don't worry about the exact spot you are to touch. Simply go down the rib cage in between the bones touch/holding lightly. At some point it will be necessary to switch from left finger pads to thumb. It is safe and loving.

Step Three: Keep your left hand thumb on the rib space under the left arm and move the right hand finger pads to the inside center of the left foot.

Figure 12: Middle Inside of Foot

You may have to prop us with pillows or sit in a recliner chair arrangement for this. Arrange yourself however is most comfortable. Hold here for a few minutes, waiting for a deep breath or shift towards relaxation.

Repeat on the other side with opposite hands.

When the green energy of the heart is free, the Blue Door swings open to the impulse of love.

THE BLUE DOOR

The color "blue" vibration frequency of free vocal expression is physically located in the throat area, ready to express the freedom you have discovered to say "no" or "yes" in accord with the heart. The correlating sound is "uh" as in "enough." There may have been many authentic heart prompts to say "yes" that have been missed due to simple tension misinterpreted. The Blue Door release helps relax the muscles needed for voice freedom and saying "yes!" to the heart's message.

Step One: Place left hand finger pads (LH-fps) on Left side of neck area in vertical line with the ear lobe. Touch/hold the right side of pubic bone with the Right hand finger pads.

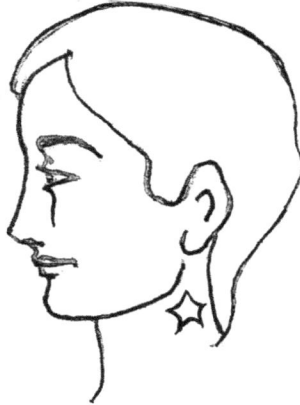

Figure 13: Side of Neck

Figure 14: Side of Pubic Bone

Step Two: Sing the sound "enough" or hum the sound and

think of the word "enough." Hold this dual energy station touch arrangement for a few breaths until you notice a shift in energy towards relaxation.

Repeat on other side with opposite hands.

Others are drawn to the vibrations of a free vocal sound. Matching frequencies resonate together and make beautiful music. Our relationships with others find confidence in the free flowing energy frequency of the Orange Door area, described next.

THE ORANGE DOOR

The color "orange" has an energy frequency that correlates with the vibrations of the lower abdomen and the reproductive capacity of the individual. The vocal sound "ooh" as in "zoom" correlates with this area of the body and its energy. Sometimes our own plans have to give way ("zoom") to the larger purposes of God. Releasing the Orange Door energy helps this happen. Our peace, joy, love, health, venue and material resources are God's area of control. When the blessings of God arrive as physical loving or a big belly laugh, stuck energy moves. Pending this event we can simply follow our Life Protocol and practice the Orange Door Release .

Step One: Place your RH-fps over the heart area in the center of the chest. Simultaneously place your LH-fps on the area in front at the arm/shoulder joint (it will be on the pectoral muscle).

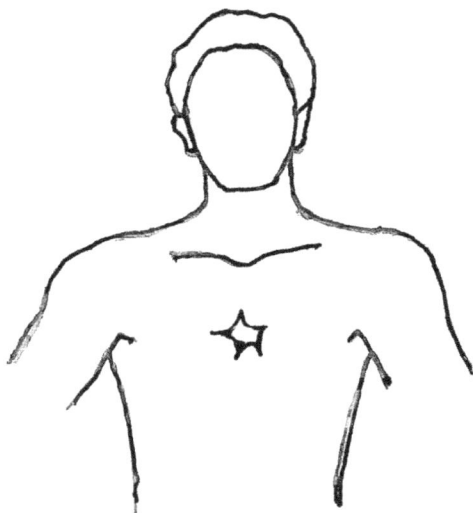

Figure 15: Center of Chest

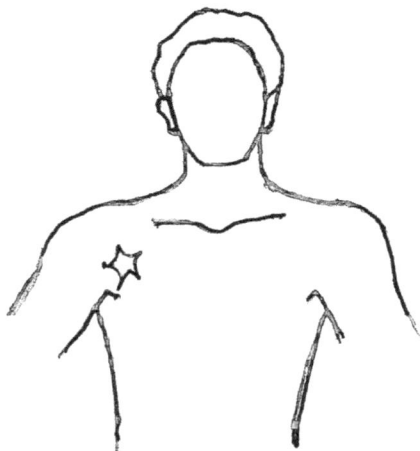

Figure 16: Front Arm/Shoulder Joint

Hold gently and breathe normally while singing or thinking the sound "zoom." Hold and wait for the pleasant shift towards relaxation.

Step Two: Move the LH-fps to the side of your left pubic bone.

Figure 17: Side of Pubic Bone

Simultaneously move the RH-fps to the Left front arm/shoulder joint area on the pectoral muscle. (see Figure 16) Hold gently for the shift towards relaxation, while softly singing or thinking the sound of "zoom."

Step Three: Place your RH-fps on the palm of your left hand, hold gently, sing and notice your energy. This potent energy station is a message center for all functions of the body.

Repeat on the other side with opposite hands.

Figure 18: Palm of Hand

These Releases become natural and easy with practice. They are good for anytime you feel tension or stress and particularly when you wake up in the morning. When in public, the palm press alone, can be used discreetly give a sense of calm.

THE RED DOOR

The color "red" has the electrical frequency and spiritual vibrations present at the base of the spine. The vocal sound is "ohm" as in "dome." Tension here may mean the current venue of our life is not home. This relates to our physical home. We don't feel like "putting down roots" where we are when the energy of the base of the spine is restricted. This sense of our natural "place to be" is a real part of life. The love impulses of body and soul resonate with particular areas of this planet and not with others, for reasons far beyond the conscious awareness. This area of our venue is God's for this very reason. There is no way for us to make a rational choice to determine our proper home or venue because of all the factors involved beyond our control. By meditating and practicing the Red Door Release, we can find peace and insight—even surprising clues and unexpected direction. Meanwhile, simply follow your Life Protocol and practice the Red Door Release to make the best of where you are now.

Step One: Place your RH-fps on the Left forearm muscle just under the crease. Simultaneously place your LH-fps on the Right forearm muscle, just under the crease.

Figure 19: Forearm Under Crease

Hold gently and sing or think the sound of "dome" quietly until you enter the zone of free vibrations, then you may enjoy singing louder.

Step Two: Leave your RH-fps on the Left forearm and place your LH-fps on the Left side of pubic bone.

Figure 20: Side of Pubic Bone

Hold/touch gently for the shift in tension level towards relaxation while singing "dome" if singing is comfortable. Notice how your energy feels and shifts after a few minutes.

Step Three: Leave your RH-fps on the left forearm and place your LH-fps on the tip of tailbone. This placement usually requires a turning of the body but it is worth the tiny bit of awkwardness. The free vibrations at the Red Door are helpful to all the body functions.

Figure 21: Tip of Tailbone

Hold/touch gently while singing "dome." Observe the energy feelings here and the opening of flow.

Repeat on the other side with opposite hands.

This release for morning or any other time of day or night, gives a feeling of composure and reminds me that "self blessing and pushing" are fruitless. The crossing of arms and touching the opposite forearm with finger pads like an Indian Chief is the picture of purposeful waiting. Our Creator has set in motion blessings beyond our imaginations when we follow his laws. At other times we are blessed, often by Grace and sometimes by intervention. He is the Root of our existence.

The next door is to our conscious awareness and intuition. When the Purple Door to our intuition and insight is opened by a surge of energy from beyond the Red Door, all are things possible.

THE PURPLE DOOR

The color "purple" (blue violet or indigo) has the electrical frequency and spiritual vibration of the energy station at center forehead just above the eyebrows, called by some the "third eye." This color resonates with truth in the form of intuition, insight and awareness. The sound for the third eye and purple is "ih" as in "high." Feel free to make up a melody or just sing "high" on one "note."

All the releases that precede the release of the purple energy station, give support and warmth to balance and materialize the truths that become conscious when the third eye opens. Opening this station helps release from the body the build up of energy and cell memory that is ready for the recycle bin. The Purple Door and its companion, the White Door creates our fountain of youth. Old cell memory makes us old. The purple color vibrations modulate into a lighter and lighter violet until they become pure white, a combination of all colors. Releasing the energy from useless and negative cell memory freshens our mind, body and soul. In contact with God through the purple and the white energy stations, we can release the cell memory that does not serve us. It is a spiritual event that materializes in the body. You may enjoy visualizing a shower of white light carrying unwanted cell memory upward and away to be neutralized by infinity. Chapter Eleven here contains a revelation about cell memory. In the Holy Zone we have no need for the armor or prompts of cell memory. The intense presence of the Lord of Life assures us that every truth and resource we need is there present and available to feed and lead.

Step One: Place your RH-fps just under the center of the collarbone.

Figure 22: Under the Collarbone

Step Two: While gently holding this collarbone area, place your LH-fps at the area on the left side of the spine just under base of the skull between the two large muscles that attach the head to the shoulders. Hold these two stations gently and wait for a shift towards relaxation.

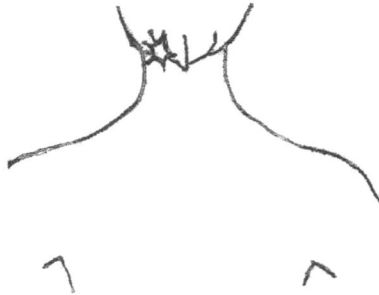

Figure 23: Base of Skull Between Large Muscles

Simultaneously hold these energy stations and sing the sound of "high" quietly at first until your voice finds resonance in the "holy zone" of sound and lets go like the flight of a bird. Breathe normally.

Repeat on the other side with opposite hands.

Step Three: Place your RH-fps on the energy station at the right side of your neck in line with the ear lobe.

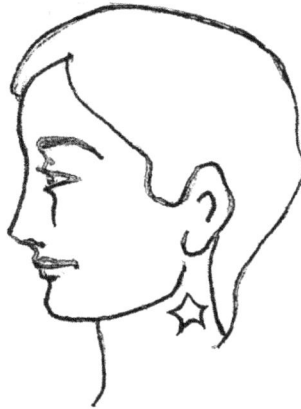

Figure 24: Side of Neck

Feel for the tension area and hold gently.

Step Four: Keeping your right hand at the side of the neck, move your LH-fps to the sensitive area just under the ear lobe itself. Sing the sound of "high" quietly on any note you desire.

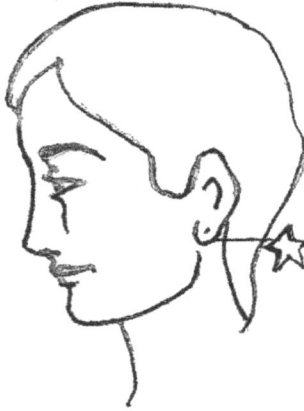

Figure 25: Behind Ear Lobe

Wait for the shift then move the LH-fps up to end of the left eyebrow.

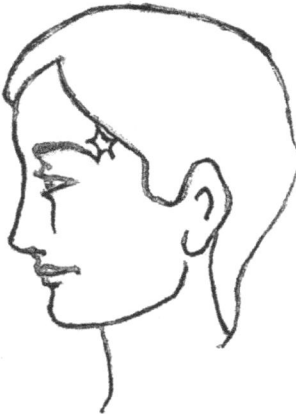

Figure 26: End of Eyebrow

Wait for the shift then move the LH-fps up to the energy station just over the center of the left eyebrow, holding gently and noticing your energy quality and movement (e-motion).

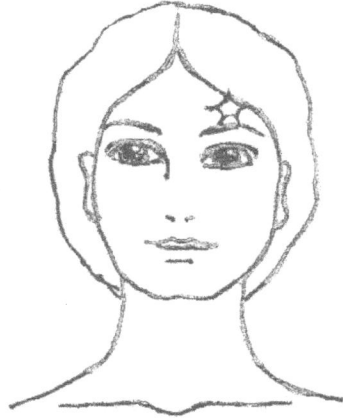

Figure 27: Over Eyebrow

Repeat on the other side using opposite hands.

The White Door (pale violet to white) is ready for entrance. Some unexpected revelation of truth is most likely to show up about now, if you are still awake!

THE WHITE DOOR

This is the finale. We now enter the White Door to higher levels of the Spirit. This energy station is best lightly touched as the brush of angel's wing. It's at the crown of the head.

The color "white" is actually a total of all the colors on the spectrum of light and has the spiritual vibration giving awareness that we are connected with God. Pale violet is next to white and complements the energy in a mysterious way. I was walking one morning in late summer and on the side of the road was a patch of wilderness where large white morning glories were growing. I had a camera with me and took a picture. When I returned home

I looked at the picture on "zoom" mode and found a beautiful pattern of pale violet all through the white morning glory flower radiating from the center, a strong violet color. This was a coincidence but like all coincidences, on purpose. Thoughts about this flower keep coming back to me. A wild flower is an unexpected blessing from God that seems to say, "Hello, I am with you!"

The energy frequency of white is the "sound" of silence. Meditation is ultimately white sound and space, permitting the Divine messages of love, truth and coherence to materialize in our bodies and our environment perfectly.

Step One: Place your right hand over the crown of your head with finger pads or palm lightly.

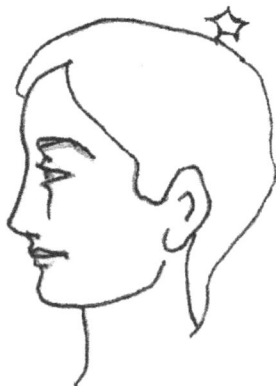

Figure 28: Crown of Head

Step Two: Simultaneously place the LH-fps on the area at the center of the forehead just above the place where the eyebrows would meet if they grew together. This place is called the "third eye" in eastern energy science.

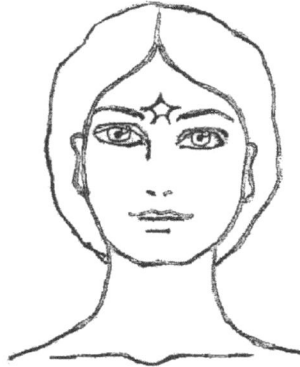

Figure 29: Third Eye

The Yellow Door makes way for the Green Door to open, which makes way for the Blue Door to open, which makes way for the Orange Door to open, which makes way for the Red Door to open, which makes way for the Purple Door to open, which makes way for the White Door to open. These Doors of energy release open in sequence naturally, yet can be used in whatever order feels right to you. Sometimes one energy station is stuck because of a greater resistance to flow in another. Beginning with the release of the Yellow Door (solar plexus) helps all the stations to give up resistance and flow. Sometimes the Yellow Door is all I need. When I have the patience or need to open all of them, the primary reward is relaxation and peace that goes from the top of the head to the feet.

The Seven Doors to Energy Freedom is a loving, self maintenance program that allows the body to participate in meditation, helping the mind and spirit to wait while God is preparing your next blessing.

The next chapter is like your good and true friend—one that will help keep you from trouble and not say just what you want to hear—the Don'ts of Life.

6

The Don'ts of Life

My Do(s) are friends that will not betray or mislead me. My Don'ts are friends too. Like the do(s)—they keep me out of trouble. I made up a rhythmic ditty to easily remember these admonitions:

"Don't worry, don't fear, don't criticize or shop.
Don't promise or over tell your truth.
Don't over nurture. Don't eat much meat.
And Don't forget your Daily Do's.
Don't fret over knowing your purpose in life.
Don't fret over how or where you'll live.
Don't let the Devil steal your joy with lies, or make you believe you have nothing to give."

They came to me all at once and have changed very little since the day I received them. Life is more efficient when we have a valid list of don'ts and observe them. The reasons for mine are settled and shared with you herein below. Since the don'ts involve breaking some major habits, I make some mistakes every day, but keep on trying. My do(s) and don'ts help me with quick choices—the times I have no time to think the situation through.

May you be directed with a special resonance as you explore the following discussion of Don'ts. Yours may be different, although I believe the ones given to me are universally valid. I pass them on to you, as I received them. The Do(s) and Don'ts are about efficiency—efficient use of the daily energy we have to express our unique love materially in this world, and have time left over for pure fun. By making your own list and practicing your personal don'ts you will understand how much time and energy is saved. With personal rules for life, day and night, there is a sense of structure that encourages relaxation and an absence of "floating" guilt. Tension and guilt use large quantities of energy that could be directed into something chosen.

The Do(s) and Don'ts are guardians of our personal allotment of power each day and guard us against negative energy and emotions. We best know what human beings are designed to do at what time of day, and learn our individual non-negotiable needs to avoid wasting the daily power pod. One of the Don'ts on my list is: Don't Neglect Your Daily Do(s).

All around we can see human beings trying to avoid natural rhythms and laws. We can (as in "able") contravene Universal laws and rhythm to suit some artificial agenda, but this causes tension in the human body, mind, and spirit. We make things happen that require fixing later in the process. Everything under the sun has designed-in laws that govern its function. We are not outside of Nature. Our instincts give us clues, yet the world we live in deceives us at times into believing we can or should circumvent natural rhythms and our inborn needs to get "stuff", look attractive, or for a temporary "feel good." We can miss sleep and eat unwholesome food if we want to, but there is always a cost. The price we pay is not always immediately apparent, but it is eventually collected. We can drink mineral deficient, impure water and stay hydrated, but the bones and body filters are taxed. When we do morning things at night and night things in the morning, a tension builds within us. Tensions use tremendous energy just existing. Once we know the truth: that we have laws and they relentlessly demand observance—we can find relief and restoration in change. We can adjust and rearrange everything in our lives that conflict with natural laws and the natural needs of our bodies, minds and spirits, if we want to, and if we care for ourselves. To care for others we first care for ourselves. Then we can teach others how to care for themselves and pass the insight on.

Knowing what to do and what not to do is a major stress reliever if it is a Protocol we agree to and participate in creating. I share a "great simplifier" with you in the next Chapter entitled "Who Controls What." I explore in Chapter Seven how the Left hand fingers prompt what we are designed to personally and actively manage; while the Right hand fingers prompt situations and events we are designed to simply embrace with gratitude and respond to with appropriate action. It is a great relief to become aware of the vital areas we do *not* need to control. This concept is difficult at first to appreciate as it contravenes the way the "world" functions today.

Many of the goals our media and social trends recommend are fostered by the evil one—the Adversarial Voice. They are wrapped in glitter, sensual temptation, and intellectual sparkle. To become aware of this deception gives you the power to rebuke it and break any temporary hold it may have on your life. The Don'ts are powerful tools to use for avoiding the ways Satan has to trick us into folly. Count to ten before you "do" a Don't—this the first step in changing some habitual response. Make your own list or use mine. The following don'ts were born of experience and inspiration, not from fear. Most of what we do from fear does not help us anyway.

My personal Don'ts came to me in about ten minutes one night after being suddenly knocked down by the flu. It only lasted 24 hours but I was "flat out" sick with all the symptoms. I wanted nothing but orange juice. I will spare you the details. The Spirit of God impressed me with everything I best never do, to live efficiently and stay out of trouble. The list was long enough that I wanted to write it all down but could not sit up or write. The Spirit "said" to me "just memorize all this list and write it down when you can." I memorized it all—had nothing else to do. When I felt better, I wrote the list I was given.

The Don'ts:

1. Do not worry. It is human to worry. The higher our consciousness level, the more we can think of to worry about. To counter this feeling we can say out loud "I will not worry. It is against my spiritual laws—it is profane." Ask the Spirit what you best do to counter this feeling of worry. Doing something necessary and right in the moment, we are less vulnerable to negative thoughts. The evil one tempts us greatly with this human tendency. If Satan can get us to worry, he rocks. Worry wastes energy and time. It produces poison in the body that has to be worked out. Worry blocks joy and love. Thinking amidst worry produces lower quality solutions to difficult situations. Worry suppresses true inspiration and valuable answers. Worry blocks the Holy Spirit's advice and comfort. The practice of Life

Protocol reduces greatly the overall tendency to think negatively. You are not required to worry—it is not your responsibility. The practice of expressing gratitude counters the habit of worrying. Gratitude is holy. Any holy action counters profanity on the spot. Speak your thanksgiving out loud and let the vibrations of holiness drive away the intentions of the evil one.

2. Do not fear. Fear is Satan's best weapon to block love. When fear creeps in, rebuke the Voice, and listen to the Holy Spirit that is loving you, accepting you, guiding you and taking care of you. Pray to cancel the cell memories allowing this emotion to be present in you—forever—all the way back to the beginning of mankind's experience. Without negative cell memory fear is impossible. Jesus came to earth, lived and took on the cross, then rose from the dead to provide a way for destructive cell memory to be cancelled. This includes fear. He came to give us the way live in the present moment without the baggage of negative cell memory. More about cell memory in Chapter Eleven.

3. Do not criticize. To engage our minds with criticism is a casual and common waste of energy and time. When you criticize another person to someone else, and do it well, they will always wonder when it will be time for them to be the object of your skill. The better you are at criticism, the less comfortable people will be with you. If you must deliver a critical observation, tell it to God or do with great care and love for a pressing, present purpose.

4. Do not shop. "Shopping" is not the same as going to market for a specific purpose and making a purchase. "Shopping" is touring the market for recreation and buying things you don't need because it is fun or stimulating or a way to prove you exist. Shopping wastes time and resources. Buying with a credit card when there is no money, to get things we don't need, is profane. Credit buying creates an unsettled feeling and an unsettled account, holds promises in limbo, and disrupts the soul's peace. Shopping is easily addictive to some persons. Those who feel entitled to anything they want will be particularly challenged. The garnering of things and the game of bargains and "self blessing" is an open door to the Voice of the Adversary who delights in leading you to waste time and money. Any delay of virtuous action is a win for Satan. Tension rises while shopping and stress occurs often because we are resisting the guilt and the Voice of the Advocate that tells us to stop and go home. If you really need something and must go to the store, then go, buy it, and leave. Occasionally you may be purchasing something for someone else and some item will pop up to your attention that has your name on it—buy it if you have the money. You deserve it and many times this is something you need but could not justify going out to find, because of the rule against shopping. This is likely a blessing from God—from the Universe. This Don't is subtle. With practice you will understand and feel good about refusing to shop and know when to accept a blessing by making a purchase for your self.

5. Do not promise. Only God can promise. When we make a promise we set up a charge of energy that requires "discharging." The cell memory of the promise turns negative if we are not able to fulfill it. Sometimes life does not permit a promise to be kept—some situation occurs beyond our control that prevents us from following through. We can rightly state an intention but not make a promise. No one can control his future well enough to promise. Often you find yourself doing something reluctantly and not appropriate to the time or circumstance because you *promised*. I try to simply not promise unless it is necessary for some obvious reason related to integrity or love, as in business or in personal relationships. Promising is a form of "self blessing" that is used often to generate some kind of positive feelings towards the one promising, looking towards a future occurrence that is often not in that person's control. My mother Edie, and my grandmother Emma would say: "There's many a slip between the cup and the lip."

6. Do not over-tell your truth. This "Don't" concerns making unnecessary personal disclosures or exposures. Your body energy will warn you if you are sensitive to its advice. A stressful feeling that comes over you when telling something to another, it a sure sign you've gone too far. When you get going on a theme of truth and go too far, you know in your heart of hearts, even if the listener is polite and somewhat interested that those that care will be burdened and those who do not will be bored. We risk the unsaid "so what?" every time we tell our truth when there is no requirement by circumstance. If you must tell, tell and tell your truth, write a book like me.

7. Do not over-nurture others. Let people you care about take care of themselves whenever possible. Some women become addicted to taking care of people—especially their children. We imagine our names on all kinds of things to do for them and everyone else. The children sometimes build up a resistance to our nurturing that creates tension and is unnecessary. Children and others need to take care of themselves most of the time unless they are very young. This is how they learn confidence, skills, and obtain satisfaction in life. We deprive our loved ones of the kind of wanting that generates resourcefulness when we over nurture, and encourage the opposite of gratitude. Gratitude calms the nerves and centers the person's spirit. To know when to nurture and when to stand back is an art that "givers" best learn without delay. There will be times when nurturing is quite beautiful and appropriate. I try to wait for those times.

8. Do not eat much meat. This is a difficult number for most people because we enjoy the taste of well-prepared meat. However, the commercial processing of animal products in this day and time is unacceptable, especially when we consider that whatever energy we eat, our bodies have it to assimilate or eliminate. We present a difficult job to the body when commercially obtained meat is eaten—challenging the digestive and elimination systems. If we can find meat that is produced with intelligence and integrity and is humanely processed, a little is probably good, yet our proteins are best obtained from organic beans (seeds), vegetables, clean fish, grains, fruit and properly produced dairy. To be blunt, a killed animal is not happy and I don't want unhappy energy in my body. I love all creatures and do not need them to die to obtain my food. My use of meat for food is rare, carefully selected and prayed over. The essential energy in food and drink can be changed as in "modified", by prayer and love. Our bodies are holy and need holy food to function as designed. My friend that lives in Washington goes into the woods occasionally, where Elk roam, and claims one with a ritual of thanksgiving and blessing, processes it on the spot and takes it home to freeze for meat. This is ideal and probably amounts to a kind of integrity only imagined by even the most compassionate and intelligent of us.

It is a wise choice to express gratitude before we eat and ask the Almighty One to bless our food with love, especially when we eat meat.

9. Do not neglect your Daily Do's. This is obvious, but mentioning it here serves us well as a reminder.

10. Don't fret over knowing your purpose in life. Your known purpose in life can change from time to time, naturally. The job for today may not be the work required tomorrow. To lock oneself into a single vocation or occupation is not necessary. There are persons who spend a lifetime learning and performing a certain skill, with good effect. Others change and their work changes with them, sometimes dramatically. If we refuse to consider our options as we grow, learn, change and become aware, something that would bless us beyond imagination may be missed. If we do everything the moment calls for with the highest integrity we know, we will connect naturally with the need for our service that matches the times, our talents and preparation. God's purposes are worked out in us. Ideally we fulfill His heart's desire and ours along the way. We may never know which job we do is small or large, incidental or important. This judgment is reserved for God. The opinion of others is completely irrelevant although it is difficult to not be affected by praise or criticism. To be above the need for "strokes" or affluence is a powerful place to be and it is peaceful. We simply do what we are called by the Spirit to do or what we find must be done that no one else will or can handle. In this process, we fulfill our purpose and learn what it is. Claiming some other so-called purpose in advance may be an attempt to insure our importance. This never is satisfying. It is a spiritual mirage.

Your life's purpose is in the heart of you, in your birth package of love impulses and is unique. This purpose evolves as you become more and more aware and conscious of your abilities and your relationship to the world and others. Your mission or purpose cannot be truly authentic if you plan it without flexibility. You would be over-controlling and the optimal help of the Universe missed. How much better to set your intention to be available to work in concert with God to do whatever He directs you to do to the highest level of integrity that you know. Making "self image" based assumptions concerning your life purpose removes the joy and surprise of God's blessing and divine leadership. Having fixed ideas about your path also creates tension, because you are in the position of "promising" yourself something you may not be able to deliver. True success in life is simply tuning in to the Voice of the Advocate and following. The material rewards may be great or small, but the peace and joy is without measure.

11. Do not fret over how and where you'll live. Environment is important. It should harmonize with the Spirit—the environment of home, work, clothing and the relationships that create personal energy around us. However, if we spend too much energy trying to control and create our environment, more important things in life will be neglected. Our personal message to others will reveal a low quality of priorities regardless of what we say. Do what you can do now about the basics, follow your Life Protocol, and let the environment simply materialize as it will. This takes faith structured by the Life Protocol and a precedent of good unfoldments. When you live in this faithful manner, God's very best blessings flow to you without the obstruction of ego (self image), pride and fear, the top three emotions that block your well being. Faith in God's providence and taking pleasure in the surprise and mystery of every day life keeps us in a state of grace where anything and everything beautiful is likely to happen.

12. Don't let the devil to steal your joy with lies or make you believe you have nothing to give. Any message that comes to your heart that tells you something that denies the basic rightness of your body, mind and soul deep within, is a lie of Satan. Don't believe it for one nanosecond. Rebuke the Adversary in the name and by the power of Jesus Christ. Clear the screen of your mind in meditation, breathe deep down in the lower part of your body, sing your energy sounds of "ohm, oooh, ow, ahh, ehh, ihh, and eee" in the vocal holy zone (Chapter Ten) or however you can or just make some sound with your breath in thankfulness to the Creator in whose image you are.

The Adversary is a contrary voice to the Voice of your Advocate, the Holy Spirit. Learn to recognize the voice of Satan. He cannot read our hearts or minds but when we fall into doing the Don'ts and into leaving off the Do's of life, there is an energy that emits like red flag. When the red flag flies, Satan gets to work on us, sending demonic beings to aggravate and sends troubling lies through whatever agents available to extinguish the fire of inspiration and joy wherever it affects us. Joy is a priceless kind of energy—responsible for the best in art, music, invention and all other regenerative works of man. It cannot be purchased. The feeling of joy makes us able to give the kind of love that exactly fits the needs of others. Joy is a noun. Love is a verb—the response to being in contact with God. When we practice Life Protocol and notice what happens, we become attuned to the lead of the Holy Spirit. The static is gone and the Voice of your Advocate is clear. The more we practice, the easier it is to hear this quiet and comforting prompt.

In all of this we live, move, share with others and express the mystery—the absolute mystery of life that remains and always will remain with God.

7

Who Controls What

We are designed to control and manage some areas of life to the most precise level we have time for in a day. This is called "taking care of business" or "self care." Other particular areas are designed to remain free as much as possible for the Universe—God, to handle as only the Universe—God, can. Our part is to embrace with gratitude and appropriately respond. I use the Left hand fingers to remind me of the areas I am to actively control and the Right hand fingers to prompt the areas that are God's. Those who learn the difference and show the difference in daily life, demonstrate a peculiar *holiness*.

To think of the Left hand as the "controlling" hand is a bit strange, unless we can see that the Left hand activity has a way of stopping us from trying to make things happen that we imagine will benefit us, but are in the providence of God. The left hand prompts us to resist "self blessing." When we try to go too far to bless our selves, the effort delays or blocks the superior blessings of God. I use my Right hand fingers to remind me of the vital parts of life to release. As we open our hands and hearts to divine potential and let go of consternation regarding our life and work *venue, health, love, peace and joy, and material resources*, and simply take care of our Life Protocol—patiently watching these areas of divine control play out naturally, our lives begin to demonstrate holiness. The more we try and control and manage these "free" areas of life, the more problems we create for ourselves. There is often perplexity here because we, the starry crown of creation, are vulnerable to deception. We have been taught by our society to dominate everything we can and to accumulate power, wealth and above all—to win. We are tricked by the voice of the Adversary into grasping for what we have no business reaching for, and leaving off what we are meant to take charge of and do—in a vain attempt to "self bless." We can take care of ourselves but we cannot bless ourselves. Only God can do that. The Adversary attempts to convince us through various methods, that we can and should bless ourselves. Grace and intervention by the Almighty is always present as we grow to understand, and daily gratitude is in order for this blessing. However, as our eyes are opened to "Who Controls What" and act accordingly, we can peacefully watch God bless us beyond anything we could do for our selves, with the *divine facility* that seems like magic.

***

As we work with the concept of leaving to God the areas divine blessing, our body automatically begins to adjust and rearrange our tensions. More and more we feel free to be who we are without effort or constraint. Everything begins to show this change—our facial expressions, our clothes, our food, our home, our yard if we are fortunate enough to have one, our way of working—everything—even the sound of our voice changes. When we live in the Zone of Holiness, we do not force our voice to make sound when we sing or speak. This concept is explored in Chapter Ten entitled "Voice: A Catalystic Frontier."

When I discovered "Who Controls What" everything in

my life began to change. A life structure made of what to do and what not do each day was essential. I needed to be consciously aware of my life structure. I recorded what I learned on paper. I was relieved to find the rules that applied to me; yet, that was only part of the distance left to go to where I wanted to be. The structure of life—Personal Life Protocol—is larger than a list of Do(s) and Don'ts. We have five areas of *our own control* correlated with the Left hand fingers, and five areas that correlate with the Right hand fingers, to *leave be in God's control*. Each one of the Left five fingers prompts an area of control; and each one of the Right five fingers prompts an area of God's control to remember. The next Chapter details the fingers and their correlations. In this way I remember the order of holiness and avoid profanity. I need no manual—all the prompts I need are with me all the time—my hands and fingers. This rather peculiar system came to me all at once, as many of my unusual revelations tend to do. It was easy—I only had to embrace the concept of "ten finger" prompts for the precepts of holy order and be thankful. I wrote it all down quickly as soon as possible. It has not changed in any significant way since the day it was revealed to me.

As I remembered and followed the Life Protocol laws and rules that I learned to rehearse on my ten fingers during times of meditation, I expected to live with peace, freedom, and blessings. The laws and rules would become my conscious nature, surely as they are my unconscious nature. They would give me security as I navigated through this world. This new simplification and new awareness of "Who Controls What" with finger prompts, was a big help in finding coherence and detachment. This all was quite good. However, soon I knew that *something else was missing*. I prayed for an answer, experimented with what I had already, and waited. The Spirit soon instructed me as described in Chapter Ten. The missing piece next needed for completing the puzzle was found.

***

I discovered that using *voice sounds* to work with my energy maintenance system (described above in Chapter Five) caused the intended release of stuck energy to happen immediately when the voice was vibrating in a particular way. This "particular way" I have identified as the zone of "holy sound." When I began to understand what happens to the body when we make free, resonant sound with the voice, it became the *first part* of my bodywork every day. In Chapter Ten the nature of vocal resonance "therapy" is explored. By Spirit revelation again, what appears to be such a vital part of managing life here on earth, came to me only a few months before this book was completed, after working on it for seven years. The Voice and its affect on the health of our bodies was not the final revelation. The most important revelation of all, cell memory and the intervention of Jesus Christ in the evolvement of mankind is explored in Chapter Eleven. I present what I have found with a sense of awe. All the other revelations simply give help in following the truth of Jesus in a world such as we live in.

The concept of "who controls what" gave me the perspective I needed for looking at all of life in a simplified way. I prayed, read, experimented and received more and more revelation on the subject I call the Personal Protocol for Life. I considered and wrote down the bounty. The word "Laws" I define as the non-negotiables that apply to all mankind. The "Rules" are guidelines that make life easier for me if I follow them. Rules are personal and customized to my individual design. I practiced the laws and the rules, journaling the reasons revealed to me as I wrote the manuscript for this book.

The Do(s) and Don'ts are tucked inside the over-all personal Life Protocol and are prompted by the Left middle finger–Do(s)—and the Left ring finger—Don'ts—in meditation. The personal Life Protocol, however, is much larger than Do(s) and Don'ts. Life is more than what you do and what you don't do. All the fingers and their correlations are described in Chapter Eight following entitled "Ten Finger Friends Meditation."

***

To experience the comfort and power of my personal Life Protocol I gently hold each finger, allowing the tip of the finger to be at the palm of the hand, at meditation time, beginning with the Left thumb, and let the Spirit that created the protocol and the Ten Finger prompts—speak.

8

Ten Finger Friends Meditation

Using the hands and fingers to remember is nothing new. It is said that we are to "tie a string around our finger" to remember. We don't need strings to meditate, but our hands are our great helpers. I call my fingers my Friends that always stay close. The division of Control—Who Controls What—I have learned to remember and rehearse on my ten fingers with gratitude being the beginning of the meditation, using my Left thumb.

Why (my conscious reasoning) Ten Finger Friends Meditation was created:

1. The need for simplicity.
2. A desire to share something that children of any age can use to calm the mind, body and spirit.
3. To prompt appreciation for the Universal rules for dwelling in the Zone of Holiness.
4. To avoid profanity.

Using the finger pads to move energy as in Acupressure and like methods, helped me to feel comfortable and natural using my hands and fingers for meditation and prayer. Sometime I simply hold the fingers, one at a time, and think nothing. The subconscious and automatic responses of the body and spirit accomplish much.

Our ten fingers represent the Left hand for man's work and the Right hand for the work God reserves for Himself. The method of energy adjustment I personally use is a combination of everything I have learned that is helpful to me and to the others that I help. The following is my meditation routine, three or so times a day. Sometimes I fall asleep with one finger in a gentle grasp. Be easy on yourself. This is for you. It is "self *care*."

I sometimes sing songs or sounds in the "holy zone" as I hold each one of the fingers, beginning with the left thumb, on any note I choose. The voice resonance works as a catalyst to release stuck energy. Think focus on right side of nose bone and belly, forgetting you have a jaw or tongue or throat at first. When the resonance is open and free, add the personal expression with lips, tongue, and by moving the jaw a little forward. Have some fun.

My left Finger Friends prompt the following messages as I gently hold each one for a few minutes. The messages and the finger correlate to everything, but no need to pin it all down unless such a need becomes your personal "assignment" from the Universe. So much happens automatically when we move with the flow of God.

LEFT HAND IN MEDITATION:

Left Hand Thumb—Gratitude: Be thankful for what you have. In the morning when you wake, at noon when you rest and at night when you lie down to sleep—thank God for what you are pleased to have—the small—the big—each thing you think of until you feel done. Tell other people "thank you" for ways they bless you. Be generous with expressions of gratitude. This attitude opens us an avenue to receive even more blessings. You have the power to transform your endocrine system for good with gratitude and Vocal Release. Hold the entire left thumb gently with your right hand. Remember that Gratitude helps to displace worry. A cycle of blessing begins with Gratitude.

Left Hand Index Finger—Responsibility: Take the responsibility that you are assigned specifically and leave off doing what belongs to someone else. There is an old saying "don't stir someone else's pot." It's a good one. To deny responsibility without your name on it, is to allow someone else to fulfill his. We are to deny responsibility—not through laziness or selfishness but to be sure we are not usurping someone else's assignment and leaving ours undone.

There is much satisfaction in accepting a job that no one can do better, or that no one else is willing to do and you see the job is vital to be done. When we deny responsibility that belongs to us, individually, we deny ourselves satisfaction although some sort of relief may be ours for a while. To accept the responsibility that has our "name" on it is a demonstration of integrity, although at first it may appear difficult, overwhelming or impossible. To accept only a limited responsibility for a particularly time is not only acceptable, it is essential. To take on too much responsibility ties up our energy and shuts off the power. The Holy Spirit will help you know what to do if you ask.

When you volunteer to accept the responsibility that properly belongs to another, who will take on yours? Do the work or project with your name on it and consciously reject another's. If you do another's work, that person is deprived of the satisfaction of performing his/her special job. The discernment required to master this control factor is subtle. You will become better at it as you consciously and with integrity, practice denying responsibility that is not yours. This may sound harsh, but it is in fact one of the kindest things you can learn to do. Some people who are not natural nurturers, or who are lazy, have no trouble with this law. Others who are born to nurture and/or "take charge" have more challenge with denying responsibility.

When you are busy with your special job you don't have time to be afraid. It is an antidote to fear and worry and frees the energy that these negative emotions consume. When you are busy doing your very special task, you simply will not be worried about who notices or what your rewards will be or how your hair looks. There will be no fear that you won't measure up. You will know in your spirit that no one can do it better. You have been prepared. Hold that left index finger until you feel a pleasant change in your body, neck or head prompting a deep breath. Listen in your spirit closely and quietly, as the message may be subtle. Remember that your have a daily allotment of power. Use it for your own responsibility. Let other people use their power to do their jobs.

Having a daily structure of laws and rules helps you to always know what to do. With you Do(s) and Don'ts handy, you will rarely be "clueless."

Left Hand Middle Finger—Daily Do(s): The left middle finger prompts me to remember that we best know what human beings are designed to do at what time of day, and learn our individual non-negotiable needs to avoid wasting our daily power pod. The Daily Do(s) are discussed in detail in Chapter Four above. Sometimes in meditation I recline and consider how I have managed the Do(s). If I am out of order I think about how it feels and how I can correct. The Do(s) are my internal life-coaching Friends. They are Friends that enjoy my success and forgive me when I miss the mark. The Do(s) were developed over a year or so of noticing what order seems appropriate and what order works best at different times of day. Each time of day has a peculiar quality of energy that calls for different doing or not doing. Listening to the advice of God's Spirit and taking notice of my own body and spirit's needs and reactions to the day's energy, helped me create the Do(s). Basic human circadian rhythm and the other natural laws of mankind provide instruction and momentum for the order of our Do(s). They are all practiced in chronological order as doing the first one sets the stage for the second one to work better—on and on. If I try to eat breakfast before bodywork, the bodywork is more difficult and the focus of the body's attention always goes to digestion first, weakening my focus on the bodywork. This is the idea. To personally adjust the order is sometimes necessary. For example, I have to shower before going to the park to walk or to work outside. Going outside fresh feels good to me. Other people have no problem leaving off the shower until the bodywork is done. I take a shower before and a shower after bodywork. That is my personal way. I use skin oil to compensate for all the extra showers, and a natural soap for shampoo.

As we practice the laws and rules of our life and follow the Spirit beyond the Rules, we will discover our true Self, our true desires, and our true abilities apart from our possessions, the opinions of the people around us, or our circumstances. Who we really are will emerge, entertain and delight and abundance will follow. This person that we really are is so much finer than any character our "ego" may construct for our perceived protection or for the expectations and entertainment of others.

With personal rules for life, day and night, there is a sense of structure that encourages relaxation. Tension uses power that could be directed into something chosen—something wonderful.

Left Hand Ring Finger—The Don'ts of Life: I remember my Don'ts as I hold my Left ring finger.

Do not worry.
Do not fear.
Do not criticize.
Do not shop.
Do not promise.
Do not over tell your truth.
Do not over nurture others.
Do not eat much meat.
Do not neglect your Daily Do's.
Do not fret over knowing your purpose in life.
Do not fret over how or where you'll live.
Do not let the devil steal your joy with lies or make you believe you have nothing to give.

The reasons and details for my Don'ts are in the foregoing Chapter Six. Yours are pending, unless found already, your notice, recordation and observance. Everyone's don'ts are deep inside, waiting to be discovered. They go with the person's design and with the human design in everyone. As you learn your identity by daily choices of integrity (holy choices), appreciation for these don'ts will grow.

When we follow the Don'ts of life and understand something of why each one is vital, we can better live without guilt. One reason we feel sad apart from events that happen, is a cloud of guilt over our hearts because of the feeling that we have done something we should not have done or missed a chance to do something right. This is held in our body cell memory. Jesus came and shed His holy blood to cancel the energy in our negative cell memories. When we accept His atonement for this heavy load of negative cell memory called "sin", there is relief from its bondage and baggage. Our load becomes light. If we follow the Don'ts and Do(s) of life, we will know what to do and what not to do and stay out of all kinds of trouble that could find us "blind side" otherwise. There is more I am sure that I don't understand about why each Don't is important, but the Spirit gave me enough reason to encourage my faith in each one. As I practice these rules I experience their value and truth. Make your own list. It may be exactly like mine, or some different. Revelation will come as you seek and make your list, because it is a holy choice. The little finger on the Left hand is next. If we mastered what the Left little finger Friend prompts, we could forget all the other rules.

Left Hand Little Finger—The Two Voices: At any time of decision, conscious or unconscious, there will be two Voices speaking to your spirit. One is the Voice of your Advocate, the Holy Spirit of Creation; the other is the Voice of your Adversary, the Evil One. The Evil One is known also as Satan. Jesus is reported in Luke 10:18 of the King James Bible to say: "I beheld

Satan as lightning fall from heaven." If Jesus was using symbolic expression, so be it. Satan is your Adversary force. Developing the skill of knowing which Voice is speaking to you and following the Advocate is the most important skill you will *ever* learn. Deception abounds in earthly life. We are to know what is real and what is a semblance—the knowledge that matters.

The Voice of your Advocate will speak to your impulses of love and lead you away from temptation. The Evil One speaks to your pride, ego, fear, envy and guilt—using all these emotions to send you down the wrong road for as long as possible. Delay and uninspired thought are the subtle tools of Satan. Rebuke the energy in this work of the Adversary and listen for your Advocate's message.

The Left little finger is held to remind us of the two Voices and to rest a moment to listen and discern which one is the Holy Spirit, our Advocate. The Holy Spirit is our Advocate Voice. This Voice speaks to our desire to do the right thing and to serve the well being of our loved ones. This Voice is quiet and persistent. Sometimes this Voice will lead us to do, or go or be outside the Rules of Do(s) and Don'ts. When this Voice calls, we follow. It preempts everything.

RIGHT HAND IN MEDITATION:

All things prompted by the Right hand fingers are God's prerogatives. If you hate to release control of the five most vital areas of your life, remember that to release control is also to release responsibility. If you are able to release responsibility you are able to release stress. The wiser and nobler we become, the more stressed, unless we can learn this vital lesson. More is not better in spiritual realms. The ability to say "No" to responsibilities not your own, is a primary survival skill and "secret" of a wise man's rise to beneficial power and influence.

Right Hand Thumb—Venue: God is the Universe and God takes care of all the Automatics. The fingers on the right hand will remind us of what we are to let go and let the Universe automatically handle. What a relief! The major mistake of modern mankind is to have this control factor backwards. This error of perception sends personal lives into a counter-clockwise spiritual disaster zone. Once we understand the proper order of life, corrections are easy and set up automatic blessings.

The feeling of peace exudes from being at the right place at the right time with the right people, doing the right thing for the right reason. This is the ideal state of being for mankind on earth. Happily, we have no control over this state of being. We can't buy it. It is a result of trust and obedience. I went to church all my life and heard about trust and obedience. How do we accomplish this feat on a daily basis? No one ever told me. I had to discover it for myself. This book is about *how* to trust and obey and reap the results on a day and night basis doing more or less ordinary things. Holy choices on ordinary occasions, is the path of an extraordinary life.

My Right thumb reminds me that I have almost no control over *where* I am physically. This sounds rather ridiculous at the outset, yet it is true. When we try to make plans and go to be somewhere that we believe is necessary or desirable, all the other factors enter in. We don't make this choice in isolation. The other fingers of the Right hand prompt the vital areas of life that affect where we are physically: index finger—health of our body functions; middle finger—our love relationships (who we draw and how it feels); ring finger—our peace and joy; and the little finger of the Right hand—our material provisions (money, possessions and resources). When we try to exert control over *one* of these areas *all* the others change and are affected like throwing a rock into a pool of water. Can you control the ripples? Can you control how the ripples made by others affect your ripples? The Universe controls automatically, by God's intervention, or by both.

Our best and only valid response is to accept where we are and embrace the other right hand areas with gratitude, openness to the seeds of new life in every area including new opportunities for well being, love and material abundance. We respond and follow through as the opportunity offers and indicates. It is not our plan, but our *response* that allows the good to happen for us in these right hand areas. Again, words are symbols and the largest and most vital areas of life escape definition (control) as we try to use words to express them. Take what I say here lightly, and ponder. The truth will be clear to your awareness, as you are ready to take responsibility for that which applies to your moment.

Right Hand Index Finger—Health & Well Being: We are led to believe by those who gain by our belief that we can control well being of the body with drugs and other man made substances and practices. Contrarily, our bodies are designed to self-repair and are led into coherence and health by the Creator. At times these other artificial things are useful; yet, the best we can do is follow our Life Protocol carefully and listen to the bodies we were given to hold our love and trust God for health and well being. Our bodies give us the clues we need to do actively whatever is necessary to prevent problems and to regain balance and health. God may lead you to a doctor, or even to take some kind of medicine. Follow with gratitude. What I am delivering here is the message that our basic health is created by the glorious design of our own bodies. There are circumstances when God uses those engaged in medical practice to help. These are not discounted. Take advantage but do not become dependent on the wrong resource for your health.

Right Hand Middle Finger—Love: We do not control the life and adventures of our original pattern of love impulses. If we try to, it is rendered impotent. The Lebanese poet that gave me enlightenment as a college student so well described this truth in his book *The Prophet* when he wrote: "...think not you can direct the course of love, for love, if it finds you worthy, directs your course." Let God write your love story and it will be holy.

Your love is something to give direction as you respond to its impulses. In this way you discover who you are and your unique purposes. As you follow your Life Protocol and embrace the impulses of your love, you will draw those who match the quality and requirements needed to see that love materialize on this earth. This is the ultimate adventure of life. Finding your love match, is about following the laws of God and your unique personal laws, listening and following His Voice, then trusting that your match will appear at the right time. Otherwise a person can be easily deceived by his own perceived need; or the needs and devices of others. Save yourself the trouble and go with the flow of God. Let your right middle finger remind you of this truth in meditation three times a day—morning when you awake, midday when you rest, and evening when you approach the simplifying night and the restoration process of your infinitely intelligent body.

Right Hand Ring Finger- Peace and Joy: Our ability to self bless—make peace and joy happen in our lives is limited by all the things affecting it we have no control over—the other areas prompted by the right hand prerogatives of God—venue, health, love and money. We can try to create a peaceful environment and that helps a bit, but the ultimate Creator of this state of being is God, the orchestrator of our existence. We can love when love is prompted and observe our Life Protocol and that is all. Peace and joy appears within, as it will.

Right Hand Little Finger—Wealth: Material wealth created by great effort will not produce the value in your life that you desire. This kind of wealth controls you and cramps all the areas of life prompted by the Right hand of God's control: your venue, your health, your love, and your peace and joy. Money derived from expressing your gifts in the process of following your Life Protocol and trusting God to open opportunities to respond to and embrace material abundance with thanksgiving—is the kind of money that will provide for your material needs in coherence with the Spirit and without sacrificing your best venue, health, love, peace and joy. It is the abundance of holiness.

In this world, no matter how diligently you trust and obey with faith and actions, there will be times when you simply feel bad and sad. What to do when you feel this way is the protocol of Grace described in the next chapter.

9

What to Do When You Feel Bad and Sad

"Satan attacks those next in line for blessings."
—Glenn T. King of TKM°

Most of the time we "freak out" it is due to lies of Satan, whose greatest pleasure is to rob us of joy and peace. Sometimes things happen that are just not good from our human perspective on earth. The effect of evil in this world causes pain, sorrow and disease. Innocent people suffer. Those who are responsible for causing the trouble don't always seem to reap their just rewards here on earth. At times like this, we suffer. In suffering there is a deeper truth to learn. The shoes of enlightenment fit best on the heels of pain. Enlightenment doesn't normally stop the pain, but ask for your revelation. Ask for the blessing that you need. If you don't know what you need, simply ask for a blessing from God and trust that it will come to you in some form in some way. This takes the focus off pain. Decide to wait on the Lord and see what happens. Do the best you can to trust that eventually peace will return. Eventually, the lies will give way to truth and blessings will come to you. It's not wrong to ask for blessings. It is part of the dynamic of self- care. We can't bless ourselves—only God can, but we can ask the Almighty to give us a blessing—make that request for something special. If you still feel bad and sad, take care of yourself the best you can and try not to do something destructive. Follow your Life Protocol and wait for resolution. The things we love the most we cannot control, particularly people. Events that involve other people can be affected but not controlled.

At times of distress we will be tempted to do something called "self blessing." This is when we decide to go beyond simply taking care of ourselves and move into the zone of profanity to provide something we feel will relieve our discomfort—something in God's area: venue, health, love, joy and peace, or money. The emotion is to "reach out and grab something for a quick fix." These areas are sacred opportunities to receive enormous blessing from God if we let Him do it and don't try to accomplish the blessing for ourselves. When these times come to us and they always do, they are the most pivotal of all of moments. They make a huge difference in how our lives unfold, although the choices may seem small from our personal perspective. The choice to wait and stay focused on the holy and see what God does to provide the answer to our needs is what makes the difference. This is the Holy Difference we seek—the energy frequency necessary to evolve and cause this world to evolve. Others will try, often innocently, to draw you downward. You can kindly reject their efforts and draw them upward. This is an area of spiritual warfare—the "Blessings Game."

The rewards for awareness of the "blessings" crossroads and letting God "do it" are where true abundance abides. These are times when we learn who we are. Times when we refuse to do the profane thing despite big perceived need and temptation. Have your words ready. They have great power to dissolve profanity—especially the word "No!" "I choose the holy!" "I want *God's* blessings!"

Sometimes we look in the mirror and don't recognize ourselves. We don't feel like ourselves in body and spirit. This often means that we are doing or about to do something misguided. Hold up and stop. Find a place of retreat, and lie down—a holy zone. Mentally first, then physically go back to your Life Protocol that is there for your days and your nights. Use the Ten Finger Friends Meditation. Even good paths may be untimely. Only God knows the right time to do the right thing. Feeling bad (tension) in our heart area, throat and in our solar plexus often means to stop and regroup. When we are tense, we are unavailable for blessings to give or receive. Tension means our energy is stuck somewhere. Go back to center, rest, pray, eat clean food or fast with juice or water. Go through the Seven Doors of Energy Freedom. These releases relax excess tension and therefore allow the energy of our being to flow. The answer will come without your pressing for it when the time is right.

Beyond the situation that is prompting pain or sadness, you may be needing sleep. If you are tempted to use drugs or alcohol when you feel bad and sad, try my "blueberry abstention" drink described in The Daily Do's here earlier. If you have no blueberries, a better than good drink for these times is:

1 cup of white grape juice (the concentrate plus filtered water is fine)
1/2 teaspoon apple cider vinegar
1 teaspoon honey
1/2 cup crushed ice
A few leaves of fresh basil

Combine in a small blender until smooth, pour into a nice glass, sit outside in nature, and have a pity party that is healthy.

The "abstention" is magic of some nice kind. It contains various, quite different plant energies (compounds) which resonate together and form a new entity of a higher order than any of them are alone.

The Red Door Energy Release, particularly, helps to synchronize your energy with the Nature you are sitting in, creating a feeling of being "grounded" and part of everything good, not separated and lonely as you may have felt before.

Alcohol and drugs make things worse. Just say "no!!" then substitute the "abstention" that tastes like wine but isn't. The ingredients are powerful and create a change in your energy when you find yourself stuck in sadness and badness.

We often have good ideas and motives but the timing is off. This gives us the feeling of malaise or the blues. Wait on God and trust for His peace to come back into your heart. We cannot create peace. It is the gift that comes from following our true love pattern with integrity, of patience and stillness, and of being in communication with those you love. Walking in nature helps to handle anxiety. The energy of nature is harmonic and orderly. It supports our best. A walk in nature is something like being in communication with Someone you love and who loves you too. We can expect others to love us, particularly when we have learned to love ourselves—but we can't depend on it. If we *depend* on others loving us for our joy and peace, we become distressed if they don't show it like we expect. Some people with a craving for drama get mad, mean and manipulative. Being mad and mean for over a few minutes is really stacking the unhealthy cards your way. Add the "manipulative" part and the game is almost over. The energy of "mad, mean and manipulative" sends people away... fast as lightning—the opposite of what is desired.

Let it go if you feel rejected and unloved. So what? Think of it as liberation from the requirement of responding. If no one throws you a ball, you don't have to worry about catching it. If you want someone to love you, pray for that one to appear and make themselves known to you. The right person for your Love will have an energy frequency that is like your own. The likeness requirement is essential. The expression "I like you" means "I am like you and this pleases me." To be with others who are like us is comfortable and it sharpens our understanding of who we are. Someone like us in spirit but opposite in body is the ultimate draw—man drawing woman and woman drawing man. The creative spark of opposites makes the "world go around." Logic enters not into this equation. To look for love with logic is like insisting one plus one is two, when in reality one plus one can equal eight thousand or more. It "depends." Wait for that person to show up as the Lord to provides. When your attitude towards yourself and your need is right, others are drawn to you surely as—and it may be—quantum physics.

Do a favor for person who needs it, with no strings attached and no expectations of recompense. Nothing moves stuck energy like doing something with love. Nothing blocks the flow of energy in all those energy stations in the body like doing things that depend on love for their power—without love.

Rest in the reasonableness of your quiet place until resolution happens. Again, what we love and need the most, we cannot control. When we seek fulfillment and happiness in other people, earthly pleasure, or achievement we are in a zone of profanity. Happiness is often found in those areas, but not when we depend on it and seek it there.

Remember who controls what and do what you are charged

with, leaving everything else to God. Ask Him to bless you and wait—with expectation of something good. The Universe—God—has something valuable for you to learn that will support your life. It seems that no truth every manifests and no light ever dawns, but for a need or a night to define it.

10

The Voice, A Catalystic Frontier

"Because I am a story-teller I live by words. Perhaps music is a purer art form. It may be that when we communicate with life on another planet, it will be through music, not through language or words."

—Madeleine L'Engle, *Walking on Water*

My youngest son, Nicholas, came into the world singing, witnessed by a full audience of doctor, dad, and me. He continues to sing naturally. Bach, the elder, sings for his supper and more, all over the world. Their sister Andrea, at age ten, sang before a family audience in the living room of the ancient Norwood family home in Columbia, Louisiana—her voice resonating off the wooden walls and floors so powerfully that she stopped in awe, and has quietly waited for the right time to intentionally begin to sing again—a time when she can manage all the feelings. Their dad would have to work very hard to make an inaccurate vocal sound. To sing is natural for Jim as breath. His other children—Della, Nelda and Clay—all sing well naturally. I sang of far away places from the age of two or three years, until something temporarily stopped me. God created song in man to give him a way to profoundly affect his mind, body and soul and those around him. The voice is our primary creative resource—ready to use at birth.

Using the voice to activate release of stuck energy came to my notice towards the end of this writing. Something was missing. There was a tension remaining despite all my adventures in turning loose everything I didn't need. I discovered and followed the basic laws of circadian rhythm, natural human life, and practiced the spiritual laws I had found. I dropped a big load of stress, yet there remained some at times, stifling tension. I felt that there was a part of myself I had never met. I wanted to meet me before someone else did. I feared singing, even speaking at times, when another person was listening. There was a voice inside I had not heard. This part of me was behind a closed door in the area of my throat. In ancient philosophy, the throat energy is said to correlate to the color blue—an aqua blue.

My aqua blue door seemed to be locked. The amount of tension in the throat was sometimes so intense that I was looking everywhere for clues to solve the uncomfortable mystery. The problem, as usual, became my teacher. Colors powerfully affect us on a subconscious level. I pondered aquatic blue.

What was that "something else" necessary to get beyond this tension level keeping me from my voice? It kept me from being and knowing myself. It felt like a closed door beyond which there was something mysterious that awaited my discovery—something I needed to move to the next level of change. A "chance" advertisement at the top of my email page caught my attention. I resisted the impulse to follow the link. One voice said "this is just another con man wanting your money" and the other Voice said "check it out." I checked it out and found just what I needed—a timely collection of information and inspiration.

The advertisement introduced a singing coach residing in California. His method offered a natural way to release tension in the human voice. I ordered the program he offered on video discs and watched it at home. This method confirmed what I had always believed about singing. Vocal release is about efficiency— using the right muscles and only the necessary muscles to make the sound of the mind and heart. Everything else is relaxed, permitting maxium vibration (resonance). I understood the theory but had not been able to apply it to my singing. The study of voice is like the study of life: get the focus right and everything else opens up to support it. It takes courage to follow your true focus when it means to quit habits formed over many years. My throat and voice muscles were "armored" as my Jinshindo° Acupressure teacher would say. Armoring has various causes. The bottom line however, is fear or restriction caused by God's timing. My courage was weak but determined like the wings of a butterfly.

I was settled on the idea that structure is necessary and it was created in my life by following some rules that came to be mine with prayer, reading, experience and revelations from out of the "blue." The area of voice is no exception. Every entity has built in rules for its use. Even my heavy blue ribbed cotton placemat at the table is best used lying flat and clean. Try and use it for a pillowcase and the result would be disappointing. Misuse of electricity causes trouble. The greater the power of the intended use, the more trouble when it is misused. The laws that govern our personal design are non-negotiable. When we follow these laws, we have a great opportunity to enjoy the benefits of the human predisposition for health and joy. One part of this predisposition is the joy in sharing with others. One of the primary ways we have to share with others is by using our voices to say words and to sing. The power of words has been recognized throughout the ages. Some believe that words are the most powerful thing in the world. When words are sung, the power is greatest. God must have sung the universe into being!

When inner tension is felt in the area of the throat and face, there is something unsaid waiting to be spoken or sung. It is blocked—by fear or God's timing or by a combination of "bad" habits. My voice is in the category of being constrained by a combination of "bad" habits that originated with fear and probably God's timing. Now, the time is right to change those habits and make them "holy." Now the message from God's Spirit is to sing and speak with freedom. I am not afraid to sing or speak now, but because of habit, I find myself in the fear mode when someone is listening. Now I have something to say and sing that demands freedom. I am working on replacing some constricting voice habits with holy ones. When I concentrate and make the holy choices in practice, I am rewarded immediately by the physical feelings as the muscles rearrange and by the emotional feeling of joy and freedom. My voice carries truth and is believable and authentic. Over all—I am enjoying the sound and it shows. When my voice enters the "holy zone" I can't help but smile a little as I sing.

The process of discovery continued and moved into the area of voice. *Writing* words was good for me, but not good enough. I had learned about the value of touch through Acupressure and related energy works. I sensed there was something more—something perhaps even more powerful than touch to affect personal energy, health, and spiritual direction. I always knew that song and speech had a peculiar power to affect people and events but I filed it back into the "later" part of my subconscious. To bring out this file and work on it would happen when the time was right. The voice was a new frontier for me. I had something to say that required an efficient and free way to say it and sing it. I knew the vocal tension must go. The first level of help for me was this voice program I ordered from the singing coach. Through it I reconnected to the thoughts and feelings I entertained about singing in the past. It was time to follow through. When something or someone is next in line, the entire Universe moves things in line for support, using the bad and the good in human nature. The event of slavery in America is a demonstration of this phenomenon.

Vibrations of holiness were set up according to the desires of God, to replace profanity and in the process created enormous good. This history of mankind shows us how God works with the evolvement of mankind—to fulfill His heart's desires. It was no accident of the Universe that slaves were brought to America to work in the fields. He could have prevented this from happening. From the human perspective, there are evils that developed and became highlighted along the way. The wrongs of slavery are real and demonstrate what happens when profanity rules the hearts of men. Other books detail this *intense opposite of holiness.* Nevertheless, as a result of the stress of slavery, a high level of holiness in the use of Voice by man transpired. The African American culture at its best, gives us a glimpse of how human emotions can be expressed in singing and how bodies can be made strong by its vibrations as simple physical activity accompanies the song. I see in my imagination the rhythmic motions of work in the fields and hear the resonance of vocal music. In the corn and cotton fields the workers needed something to feel free that was real. This freedom was discovered by the "slaves" in singing songs of faith and love and of comfort in Jesus Christ—the ultimate source of freedom. Those who suffered the ill effects of physical and social slavery for a time, were given a great gift of freedom in song, strength of body, and in the ability to enjoy fully—particularly on the levels of orange and red energy, the simple good things of life—plus more—the gift of Christ. For this I thank God. For the demonstration of this freedom and joy to my spirit, I thank all the Americans from African descent whose lives are led by love. The energy in the negative cell memory of slavery can be cancelled. This concept is explored in the next chapter. The knowledge of Voice that I seek is fortified and strong in the cell memories of my African American friends, past, present, and future. I intend to make it so in my useful cell memory. Sometimes *feeling* free is better than *being* free. Being free follows.

***

Voice sounds best with the least control. The more controlled it becomes, the less expressive it is. Into the singing program just one day I noticed that the principles involved were exactly the ones I was working with to find freedom from stress and tension in every other area, to be myself and do all I was capable of doing and creating. The message was clear as a summer day in Louisiana: "Control what you are supposed to control and let go of the other." The vital areas prompted by the right hand fingers are beyond our control, although we are apt not to believe it. As explored in the earlier chapters here, when we try to control one of the right hand areas and get good at it, the others that we have allowed to cruise, can go amuck to disturb what we thought was settled. The applicable law here is to leave the right hand areas to God who has the power and intelligence to manage our venue, health, love, peace and joy, and our material resources. Our part in these areas is to simply embrace, nurture and maintain with thanksgiving, what God provides and orchestrates. This is subtle, and the successful use of this life skill depends on the individual's level of awareness. It is the knowledge that matters and comes with insight, practice and experience.

In the area of voice, we use the mechanical protocol for making a pure sound, do only what is necessary and leave the "glory" to God. To let go of our voice muscles and focus on a very small area of control, takes a willingness to let go of pride, ego and fear. Some fortunate ones have been encouraged to do this from early childhood by example and by wise parents and teachers. Some even have a store of good cell memory from their ancestors that brings them into the world singing with a natural power. With awareness and practice, these blessed ones can learn to sing better than natural. I was determined to let go and allow my voice to be. To release more than sixty years of armoring, was not and is not easy. Now it is necessary. No turning back. I committed to learn the designed-in rules for using my singing voice. The speaking voice, I expect, will also improve.

Time will tell just what this new opportunity for vocal freedom means to me. Voice practice is now part of my daily bodywork. It is the most important part of my bodywork. When there is time for nothing else, I practice vocal mechanics. The Acupressure releases help release the voice. The use of basic vocal rules is an area of legitimate control for intentional expression. I hope that one day it will be second nature and will not need so much concentration. At times even now it happens without concentration but rarely. To engage throat, jaw and tongue muscles the least is to enjoy singing the most. To control the part of life that is ours to work on and let go of the other and notice with surprise what happens, is to enjoy life the most.

I proceed to experience my voice with a delicate awe, knowing that once released I could not go back to being the same vocally indefinite person. When we allow ourselves the vulnerability to open the Aqua Blue Door of the voice, we can learn in depth what is behind the Green Door of the heart. Opening and discovering the voice and heart to life is a passage from semblance to substance. It is an act of will—your will to be authentic. You say to all Creation that you will not fear change. You do not fear life and the time for you is "now." The sound of your true self is about to be heard. It may be a small sound like the whirr of tiny wings at first or a sound that cracks and scoops—nevertheless, be ready to hear someday the voice of many waters. Be ready to discover your dreams. Only a shadow of them has been known thus far. Relaxing the voice muscles and becoming aware of what stands in the way of the sound behind the Aqua Door, then embracing it no matter what, may the beginning of your next level of evolvement.

These are the mechanics I have discovered in voice practice:

1. Lightly experience a sound like "uhm" or "ing" on the right side of the nose bone. This is the "mental" part of a three-fold experience.
2. Reach the focus to just below the navel in the orange area of your energy and feel for a ticklish vibration as you make the sound. Let there be "nothing" in between the blue and the orange sound.
3. When this sound feels free and good, then move the jaw very slightly forward, letting the tongue be loose and flexible. Now continue to sing with more intentional expression and more experimentation, no matter how it may sound. Drop your fear forever. Who cares if you crack?

This is practice and play time. You won't always crack. Sing into the gap if you sense one coming and play. Try to crack and see what happens. Enjoy the first part, connecting the intent of sound on the nose to the orange area below the navel—feel the tickles and forget there is anything in between. Enjoy the warm buzz of vibration and interplay of blue and orange. Feel the sound. Later, you can think about performance but not while practicing alone. Your practice is the time for fun and experimenting—getting to know all about you. Sing a song or phrase if you want to, but seek to feel vibration.

When maximum vibration is allowed, you have a chant. I never understood chanting before this voice revelation came to me. It is about feeling not hearing. Chanting and singing in the Holy Zone sends healing vibrations all over the body. It is a spontaneous face-lift by an automatic rearrangement of muscle tension—temporary at first. The lips energize with sound vibration, the jaw relaxes, the eyes open wide and the eyebrows lift upwards. Singing in the Holy Zone allows different muscles to be used that have possibly atrophied and regenerates energy patterns that show love. How much more beautiful can a countenance be, than when it "looks like" love? Someday medicine will be mostly about sound therapy—no drugs and no surgery.

Singing without fear is one of the pleasures rewarding your decision to be authentic and to seek the Holy Zone. It is a good feeling. Go for the way your voice feels, not the sound of look of performance. There is where the power resides. The Zone of Holiness is about discovering who you are by being vulnerable in all areas, not just in the area of using your voice to make sound. You can be open to your secret self, behind the Blue Door and behind the Green Door, yet secure because you follow the universal Protocol of Life, which is a set of rules for living in the Zone of Holiness. The rules you discover for yourself, if they work to eliminate stress, will be holy rules. Shackles of tension and fear will drop off when resistance is released, as the rules designed into your being are acknowledged and followed. The more tension we can release, the more easily we can come to enjoy the sound of life—singing and speaking.

Vocal tension is easily released by some, others not so easily. This release, however, is essential to fully enjoying a flow of heart energy back and forth from oneself to others. When free, the heart feels no longer alone but connected to everyone, now and everyone who has ever lived on earth, and all those who will be here sooner or later. Free heart energy is the vehicle of love. Love is the most important thing in existence. Everything that exists in life is either created by love or the suppression of love. To materialize our love is our job here on earth. When this love of ours is shown by expression of some kind or by the creation of something material, we encourage others to do likewise.

A planet of people all loving with varying frequencies and unique differences is the symphony of life. As we respond with integrity to the revelation of our own love messages—message designed into our being and given to us at birth with the breath of life—these love impulses find their way into bodies and material objects and events. Materialized individual love is visible, touchable holiness. The theme of this book is to explore how to do this with the least effort and the most joy. Peace and love all over the world is possible as person by person we enter, live in and appreciate this Zone of Holiness. The ripple effect is automatic and as powerful as the tsunami waves to eventually, level by level, eliminate profanity. The desires of man will evolve to make this happen and he will grow to be that worthy companion to God, that was planned from the beginning.

The deeper mystery of love, life and holiness will always elude us. Nevertheless, we owe it to ourselves to open to the possibilities unimagined along the way and enjoy the benefits of the Zone of Holiness. We are then as close to the source of love and life as possible and we are able to move with the rhythm and revelations that arrive daily for those who want to feel and know holiness. When practicing the holy protocol of voice and life, sharing comes naturally without trying—automatically. Finding the Zone of Holiness in the voice is required for complete personal authenticity.

My own voice opens at times into the zone that feels like a Zone of Holiness. I can't yet command it into being when I want to like the genie in Aladdin's lamp, but I describe in these words: The nose, and head area feel open and free. The eyes widen and eyebrows lift. The throat feels unengaged. The abdomen area feels a vibratory ticklish sensation. I can move my jaw and tongue in a way that seems to be coloring the sound and taking the sound to a level of personal expression. My lip muscles engage a little and I feel a slight vibration in them. This is a description of free vocal expression from the inside of the person who makes the sound, occasionally! I hope to be able to sing this way whenever I want to, but so far it only happens at times during my practice. It feels as if God is present in the sound more intensely when I sing in the Zone of Holiness. The voice is outside of my control and I like it. I feel connected to something larger than myself. Intentional living and intentional singing, with love and integrity, even when we are all alone, will join you like family to a great group of holy people. Some you know now. Others you will draw and meet. Another group will lend support to you by their very existence. Sing yourself into holiness and let the vibration move throughout your being. It will move in waves invisibly to everyone in the world, stirring up love and helping us all to heal.

11

Jesus Christ and Cell Memory

"Behold the Lamb of God, which taketh away the sin of the world."   *The Bible, John 1:29*

From my human perspective, this chapter is the most difficult of all to write for the reason that I have had no contact with any other discussion of this particular revelation. There may be other discussions published or even in the process of being written, but with searching, I find none yet with the same message. At this time I am out here alone. My authority is the Holy Spirit, the Bible, some inspiring books, and my life experience. The following is a revelation concerning Jesus Christ and the purification of our human cell memory.

Your cell memory is not who you are. The memory stored in our body cells contains good experiences, images, thoughts, emotions and information; but like a computer that has been used to go all around the internet for various reasons and has collected information and links, our cell memory stores images, thoughts, emotions and information (true and false—good and bad) from our own doings and from our ancestors and from people and events that affect us from all mankind. Each cell is said to contain a brain and filtering system that we can exercise some dominion over. However, there are cell memory factors that we cannot manage without help. All cell memories affect our feelings, thoughts and our choices. Our innocent and pure love pattern that was given to us at birth has impulses to materialize itself in this world, yet has to deal with the cell memory and overcome all the negatives.

Those that can purify their cell memory and express their original true love pattern are the victorious ones in this life. This love expression can be any form of communication, and ultimately it is expression that results in something material. This is holy creativity. That is success. Nothing else is success. Having children is the ultimate form of creativity for mankind, yet to merely participate in the conception and birthing of children is not victorious necessarily. We give our children our unmanaged and impure cell memory along with the wonderful stash. God helps them. His intervening grace and love enter into this picture even before they can choose to believe or not believe in Jesus Christ and the gift He brought to mankind. We can bless our children and all generations by purifying our cell memory and living in the Zone of Holiness.

We are free to begin this restoration now. I am impressed to believe that as I purify my own cell memory, the benefit flows to my children and future generations. Timing is different with God—different from the way we ordinarily perceive time and the effect of our prayers and actions. I suspect that someday this purification process for all generations will be a given— "scientifically" established.

The energy that supports cell memory of our own and ancestral wrongs can, by prayer and holy practices, be *discharged* because of the work of Jesus Christ on earth—the cross and resurrection. The energy holding negative cell memory or any cell memory in the body can be released. When a cell memory has no energy, it cannot affect us. A voice singing a song, without energy, does not affect us. We tend to believe almost anything that is sung or spoken with the right frequency of energy. However, if a particular bundle of information is contrary to the laws of the Universe and contrary to the purpose of the Creator (a lie), it will eventually "self destruct" no matter how powerful it may appear at first to be.

The phenomenon of Jesus on the cross was the lie of all times. He was crucified as a common criminal while being the Savior of mankind. At his departure from visible life, the earth shook violently and became dark. The veil of the temple was spontaneously torn in two. Satan was allowed to mimic truth to the minds of the local people who were confused and lacked grounding in truth. The vocal demands of the crowd were convincing and supported by the deceived clergy of the day. The way of life of the religious leaders was threatened. Change was demanded by the teachings and the very presence of Jesus. The cleric's pride, ego, fear and jealousy created anger when crossed with the love of Christ. Something had to give. A huge energy block developed in mankind that had to be dealt with no delay. The cell memory in all of mankind to that day had to be cleared.

The religious leaders of the Jews in Jesus' day led the people's thinking. The media is in that place today—radio, television, internet, films, music and visual arts. Whether or not we are aware of their power, these modalities rule the minds of those unguarded by holiness. They are not all bad, ofcourse, but the power is undeniable. The media is, in its abstract form, a tool just as thinking is a tool that can be used by the Almighty to materialize love or by the adversary to deceive and to block the materialization of love with sparkles of profanity. The adversary is always seductive.

No longer can those who live in the Zone of Holiness and claim the promise of Christ be silent when God's message of the moment is delivered to their spirits. Profanity uses the media and mimics divine light to those who have not discovered the protection and power of the Zone of Holiness called by whatever name. A rose is a rose, it is said, by any name. To sit back and allow profanity to control the media is now dangerous to the survival of mankind and this earth as we know it and desire it to become. People will follow because that is what people do. Those without a clear concept of truth and a commitment to living it are looking for something to follow. The adversary's seduction easily appears to be the answer for congregations of confusion.

If holy choice makers don't use the power, those deceived into profanity will use it and propagate destruction of life, health, strength and beauty without being aware of what they are doing. We have the opportunity and responsibility to stand up and speak, sing, paint, lead, teach—to fearlessly perform our particular job, whatever it is, with holy integrity. The Universe will be a force behind you and love will orchestrate the details beyond those you can manage. All that is necessary is your willingness and mine to make the holy choice and follow through with prayer, meditation and action. The gaps will be covered by the Almighty.

When Jesus accepted the crucifixion, shed His blood, and gave up the Spirit from his earthly body, the work was done. The gift was offered. In losing the presence of Jesus on earth, we gained the Holy Spirit to be with each one of us, as a guide to the Zone of Holiness. The mystery of Jesus remains. We are allowed to know what is necessary for our assigned responsibilities—assigned by the Universe, the totality of God. As we "flesh out" the assignment we individually have, mankind is restored and all we are intended to be, is revealed and made material. Through Jesus the fulfillment of our responsibilities is possible. Before Jesus, no one could rise above his cell memory without the intervention of God for an overriding purpose. Now everyone can be the hero their love pattern is designed to produce.

This is God's plan for saving mankind from self-destruction. The Bible contains the story of Jesus. When we read the Bible, particularly in the morning, the Holy Spirit provides the understanding we need for the moment. Beginning with the Book of John is a quick start to finding your own confirmation of the truth here. Later go back to Genesis and read as the Spirit directs. If you seek and ask for wisdom concerning something from God, you will not be disappointed. Don't expect it immediately. God has a timing all His own. Simply continue to pray (ask), meditate (receive), and trust, expecting an answer when the time is right.

The cancellation of negative cell memory may happen immediately, today or even tomorrow; however, it *will* happen when you accept what Jesus did for you and begin the journey into the Zone of Holiness. When holiness pervades your life, dispersing the perversion of profanity, the ripples you set in motion will change the world in a way that supports the holy difference. When you intend to release negative cell memory from your body, this is the beginning of transformation from the profane to the holy. If you really want to let go of impairing cell memory, it will happen and become an adventure worth sharing. The foregoing Chapters provide everyday, simple ways to claim that blessing for your self and be that blessing for others. If you haven't yet learned, you can learn to live and practice a holy difference.

God could take away the baggage of negative cell memory in the twinkling of an eye and deposit you into the Zone of Holiness, but this is not His way. There are reasons, of course, for God's way of saving you and all mankind. The displacement of negative cell memory with truth and love happens in you and in me, with prayerful intention expressed, then choice by choice accompanied by action. This way, we develop in awareness and understanding and become good companions to God.

Our good works do not save us from the effects of our negative cell memory, although the concept described here may appear to suggest that at first glance. We are saved by our faith in Jesus Christ. Jesus was questioned intensely after providing food for thousands from a boy's lunch. This feat got some attention that day. People crowded around Him with questions and it was a big teachable moment. Jesus told them about Himself and *cell memory*, without using the modern phrase, in a discussion reported in the Bible New Testament. Jesus expanded His truth with symbolism and abstract concepts with daily life imagery and parables. The spiritual eyes that were open, received the truth intended by the Lord. Others either rejected the teaching or simply found a truth on the level of their need. The following words spoken by Jesus must have enlightened and comforted some, but they disturbed the literal minded in His audience:

"I am the living bread which came down from heaven:
if any man eat of this bread, he shall live for ever:
and the bread that I will give is my flesh,
which I will give for the life of the world."

The Bible, John 6:51

Jesus—using food imagery and eating symbolism— told the crowd that to accept Him would change their eternal destiny. This process involves mysterious the human mind cannot comprehend. Faith is required. Proof is seen in our daily awareness increasing as we make holy choices led by the Holy Spirit. The cell memory of sin and wrong eventually consumes one unless the Spirit of Christ dwells in the cells of that body. The Christian journey begins by simply inviting Jesus into the cells of our body. Even this is usually gradual and noticed as we make our daily choices—confirming our reception of Christ—choice by choice. Notice the blessings that follow. Blessing you cannot create will come to you as a direct result of prayer for what you cannot do alone—in ways you cannot or dare not imagine.

As Jesus on the cross took in His body the energized negative cell memory of man (sin)—past, present and future—He became the bridge over troubled water and our pathway to eternity. Our part is to simply love Him, thank Him, accept His gift and follow Him—all the way into infinity. As we accept His sacrificial work on the cross we receive Salvation for the price of trust and obedience to the Holy Spirit, our educator, comforter and illuminator. Our life beyond earth is maintained with Christ and our life on earth transformed.

The idea that we can clear our cell memory of its impairing effect by trusting and accepting Jesus Christ, may be a leap for you, even if you were raised in the church. For you who have had no contact with true Christians, even a greater leap of intellect and faith may appear to be required. As Jesus fills our cells with His being, the energy in sin (negative cell memory of wrong, harm and lies) is discharged and cannot affect us.

Read on as the Spirit leads you and do not let a desire for simple logic keep you from complex truth. Eventually, you will see a spiritually infused logic that is entirely believable. I describe a logic that reveals the only viable solution for the problems of the individual and for mankind's survival—a logic inhabited by mystery.

I received a revelation from the Spirit in a flash as I prayed for wisdom concerning Jesus. It was not the first time I had prayed to understand Jesus. Suddenly on this day or night in 2013, the truth swept over my mind and I remember saying "Holy Smoke!" out loud. I jotted down some quick notes, then continued with my daily Life Protocol feeling amazed and thankful. I often write some time later that which I have a flash of revelation about, and the concept develops as the writing hits the page with no mental foreknowledge.

I connected the cross of Jesus and subsequent resurrection from the tomb, with the burdening baggage of our cell memory sometime in the year 2013. I knew from the time I first heard about Jesus that He was more than I could understand but I did not want be where He was not. I went to church, I read my Bible, I talked with my friends and family some about Jesus but never really understood much of anything about Him and the true significance of the cross. I had many questions and few answers, but I found myself speaking His name over and over in all kinds of situations when there was need that I could not supply.

While pondering the idea of cell memory, I was led by the Spirit to find and read Dr. Bruce Lipton's book *The Biology of Belief*. I had read about quantum physics being the physical link to spiritual science. It seemed to me that the more we learn about the physical world through quantum physics and other sciences with names we have yet to invent, the closer we will get to the spiritual world and its laws. Deepak Chopra's writings and Alexander Loyd's book, *The Healing Code*, prompted me to think more about our cell memory, quantum physics, and the possibilities for human healing in ways I had not imagined before. Then I began to think about Jesus. I had heard from childhood how "Jesus saves us from sin"—how "his blood washes us clean." There is a song "though your sins be as scarlet...they shall be as while as snow." I never rejected these promises but never came even close to understanding them, until I ran smack into the concept of cell memory. In my awareness, Jesus and science had collided.

When God created mankind He knew from the beginning what would happen in our cellular bodies as the experiences of life, both bad and good registered in human cells. He knew that we would retain deep in our cells, the memories of everything that we, and our ancestors, all the way back to the first man had ever experienced. He knew that some of our experiences would be perceived rightly and some we would perceive wrong. Some would be truth and some lies but both would affect us as truth and cause us to feel and do and be. All of this motivational energy would be in our body cells. Some would be harmonious with and would support the love pattern given to us in the form of impulses unique and identifying us; and some would be contrary to who and why we are—thus the pain and stress of life. As mankind progressed he would have more moral and spiritual and physical problems because of cell memory confusion. Satan would romp, taking full advantage of all the confusion.

We have trouble acting and feeling in harmony or sync with who we are at the core, because of cell memory. Somehow the energy in all the cell memory that offends our original love pattern must be *dis-charged*. We must find a way to deactivate cell memory that harms our ability to live with a holy purity in the present moment. Our cell memory storage contains not only our personal experience, but also that of our ancestors and all of mankind all the back to the beginning—back to "Adam." Some cell memory is good and some is bad. Some supports the materialization of our love pattern and some does not.

Even the good cell memory can distract us from embracing the opportunities of the present moment. Bad cell memory can cause us to believe we are someone we are not; or not someone we are. Cell memory that we did not create with our own choices can cause guilt we don't deserve to carry. I see that we need a Savior and we need to be saved, as the gospel preacher tells us. The reason some "new thought" forerunners find these preachers so irritating is probably because somewhere deep inside is the knowledge that they are right, despite the style they find offensive.

Jesus Christ ushered in a new day with the law of Love. If everyone were walking this earth in perfect Love, no other law would be needed. When we were born, our soul was given to each of us a package of love impulses entirely our own, like none other. Our purpose in life is to materialize that love. This is naturally done without effort in our ideal state of being. The villain is this contrary cell memory we hold from our ancestors and from all of mankind that causes knee jerk responses and choices that are not coherent with the person we really are. The cell memory held in a person's body is energized by particular situations liken to those that created the cell memory, and decisions are prompted that are often incoherent with that individual's unique and perfect love pattern. This is in the category of a "wrong choice" which is technically "sin." Some of these incoherent choices are well meant and some are not, but they impair us. Add our own "sin" to all that we hold from the past that we have not created and—without giving energy to the negative by going into all the wrongs of mankind—we obviously need help.

God knew and in our own souls we know. Something had to be done or the weight of negative cell memory would eventually destroy mankind. Something was done, according to plan. God incarnate, Jesus Christ, appeared on earth with a mission. He was and is the incarnation of atonement, once and for all. Through the Cross event, Christ took on Himself the wrongs of all mankind, past present and future, and cancelled them. This is a great mystery and will probably remain so. The atonement is done, but the acceptance and activation in each person's life is his personal choice.

It appears that people instinctively want to cleanse their cell memory of images and experiences and lies that impair their true love expression but don't know how. Alcohol, drugs, sex, work, exercise, dancing, yoga, food, shopping, tapping, saunas, vitamins, even singing—all the destructive and all the good self help things people do cannot take away the baggage of impairing cell memory. We need something that really works. If all these and other intended self blessings would do the job, why did Jesus come to earth and suffer on the cross, then rise from the grave, to save mankind? Jesus wasn't stupid. He knew what He was doing.

Man was given the opportunity to discharge his burden of sin—his own wrongs and the wrongs of all of his ancestors and mankind. The baggage of cell/soul memory was no longer a mandatory burden. A new holiness was made possible beyond keeping the law. Man was given a path back to the Garden—the original Zone of Holiness—the second time as an aware observer, with a new and infinite capacity for enjoying the beauty and being nourished by its provision. The Holy Zone is where we find everything we need, automatically, by design and beyond our means to create it. To get there we have some responsibilities to fulfill—nothing onerous—nothing that takes great effort—just a desire, a simple understanding, and a commitment.

***

For years since the birth of Jesus, the Cross and Resurrection, mankind has been allowed to seek, find, follow or flounder and has been slow to realize the need for choosing Christ, accepting His atonement, releasing the baggage of negative cell memory, and the Zone of Holiness as a daily way of life.

Facing new threats of destruction—not from God's punishment, but from his own disrespect of the environment and his fellows—mankind is at the point of necessity. We are at a place of crossing roads. The choice for man now is holiness, regeneration and peace *or* profanity, degradation, and destruction. There is an affirmation that I say to confirm the work of Christ for myself in the morning: "I release all cell memory I do not need, by the power of the cross of Jesus. It is a new day. Thank you God."

The Holy Spirit, arriving upon invitation, guards our cell memory. As we voluntarily release all cell memory that we do not need, the energy is discharged until the time comes that we need a particular memory. The Spirit then highlights the memory for our use. Old cell memory that is destructive, hurtful and harmful can, through prayer and the making of holy choices be materially expelled from the body, nevermore to affect us.

***

The highlighting of good cell memory happens at times

when we need it. I was awakened one night recently with an obsession to come up with the name of a particular movie actress. By a long process I won't detail—to stop thinking about it, I went to my laptop computer, followed some leads and found her name. She was Jennifer Jones. Looking at her profile on the internet it came back to me that in 1955 a new movie was introduced that won Academy Awards in several categories. Jennifer Jones took the cup for best actress and the title song was the Academy's choice. A picture of Jennifer Jones and her male lead, William Holden, was on a piece of sheet music for *Love is A Many Splendored Thing* that sat on my piano for years. The Spirit had during the night, highlighted for me this magic—music by Sammy Fain and lyrics by Paul Webster that won the Academy Award in 1955 for Best Original Song. I must have played it—maybe sang the song hundreds of times. It was featured on the popular 1955 television show *Your Hit Parade*. Written in the relatively innocent America of 1955, reminds me and everyone, that when all is said we know to say and everything is done we know to do, love is what matters. I remembered the poetry from many years ago:

"Love is nature's way of giving, a reason to be living.
A golden crown that makes a man a King."

I needed the simple reminder for grounding (red chakra), while dealing with so much spiritual science and the Holy Spirit knew it.

Another coincidence was an extra blessing: this song fits my simple version of the ancient stretch routine from Asia called The Chinese Essential Eight Silken Movements. I do "the eights" like a dance in my Daily Do's bodywork time. I tried the "dance" while listening to Gisele MacKenzie, star of the Saturday night Hit Parade, sing *Love is a Many Splendored Thing* via time capsule from 1955 (a video found on the internet) and found it perfect for the movements and helped me easily remember all the eight stretches. When I "sing" the song myself as I do the "dance", the stretches have so much good energy that I only need to repeat each motion two or three times during the song. The benefit is much greater than before, when more repetitions were used without singing the love song. "Thank you" good cell memory.

Good cell memory is that which supports the materialization of our original love pattern. Bad cell memory is that which stifles the impulse of our heart. Even good cell memory can be a burden in our moment of now. To be pure and holy with only the necessary cell memory, open and receiving all the blessings God has to give us right now, is the ideal state of being. The innocence reclaimed by release of bad and unnecessary cell memory, is innocence with awareness. It is holiness by choice.

***

My prayer is this, as far as words can express it:

"Thank You Jesus for suffering and cancelling all the bad cell memory (sin) that harms me and keeps me from being the Love that I am. I accept your gift of Salvation and invite you into the cells of my body. In Your name, Jesus, by the power and authority of Your sacrifice—I cancel the energy in all cell memory that I do not need. I understand that as Your being fills my cells, sin is discharged and I am restored. I understand that Your presence in my body cleans my cells and opens them for divine Blessings. I want to be different, holy and clean. I open my heart and hands to receive everything right now that you want to give me, especially the gift of being perfectly me forever. Let this prayer flow to the benefit of all those I love—even those I have yet to meet."

Our minds are probably infinite. We are more than we know. The concepts just discussed are beyond our conscious means to understand. They are mysterious and are intended by the Creator to remain so. Thanks to God we are not responsible for the mechanics of cancelling cell memory that is harmful or that we do not need. We simply claim it with gratitude to Jesus for making it possible. This is the part we receive and thankfully embrace. The active part of cancelling old impairing cell memory is to set our intention to live in the Zone of Holiness, follow the rules, and teach others. From this place we can begin to gradually discharge the energy in our offending cell memories—the bad ones containing "sin" or wrong choices and actions—and even the good ones that hold us back from needed change or fresh new life. The cancellation of cell memory energy results in actual release of body cells. Our bodies will change and rearrange synergistically according to its own esoteric protocol. We will sweat and shower. We will drink pure water and use it to move out the old and bring in the new. We will eat holy food. Our world will change and rearrange. This is an exciting time to live. Life Protocol gives us structure for day and night. Our awareness is evolving. We are beginning to recognize the holy from the unholy and the clean from the unclean. We can know what the Zone of Holiness feels like and how to stay there. We can know who we are. We are called to know that Jesus Christ is the door that leads to that which remains beyond where something new waits to be discovered. There we will have new ways to learn more about who we are and new ways to be, with others that we love to be with.

Meanwhile, we can present ourselves clean and holy in the present moment, knowing what to do next, with all the resources we need to do it, confident that we are in the right place, at the right time, with the right people, doing the right thing for the right reason.

The next and final chapter brings us back to earth with a resonant thud, where we experience something the angels have no use for...sexual expression...where opposites create dynamic power in every area of life on earth

12

Sex in the Holy Zone

Sex is God's primary creative tool. We are created in His image. The Almighty One uses sex to develop the lineage and intent to fulfill His heart's desires. His anointed ones are being created generation by generation to lead, inspire and materialize all that is necessary to show God's story to all of mankind.

Look with your heart for something beautiful and holy to which you have no resistance. This is your open door to freedom. This is your way to express your own true love. Make yourself pure and holy, discharging all cell memories that offend your original love impulses. Then and only then are your eyes open to the exact match that is now on earth for you, with whom you can create all the desires of your heart. This is the law, the grace and the truth for all generations. Selah

When looking for a mate, it is vital to cancel all unnecessary and all impairing cell memory. Being clear, open and innocent of past wrong (redeemed) attracts holiness. If a person is baggaged with sin (negative cell memory in body) from their own choices and/or from the wrong choices of ancestors and even all of mankind, all their choices are burdened. Profanity is attracted and fueled by negative past cell memory. People with qualities that fuel the energy in past problems will continue to appear and be drawn to you unless the old cell memory is purified. A venue, a state of health, a loving person, peace, joy and financial resources that resonate with your own true original love will appear in your life like magic when you release the energy in all offensive cell memory and expel it from your body. When you are ready to release all cell memory, *good or bad*, that you do not need in this moment—you are ready to experience heaven on earth. The sound of white light will vibrate throughout your body and soul. Your mind will take notice and connect the dots.

Sex is about the attraction of opposites. Sex is about love. Sex is about creativity. Sex is about man. Sex is about woman. Sex is not about animals or angels or thinking. Sex makes the world turn. On every level of sex...the physical and the non-physical... one energy frequency draws the frequency it needs for completion of the bio-electrical and bio-chemical reaction required for materializing spiritual intent.

Like draws like for support and sharpening, as King Solomon wrote in the *Bible*, Book of *Proverbs*, yet the creative spark of God happens with interaction of opposites. To speak of sex in words is profane, but for a narrow thread of permission with a high purpose. Great care is used here in this final chapter to assure a holy treatment of the most powerful force on this earth.

The power of sex is a mystery in the area of God's right hand. Venue, health, love, peace and joy, and material resources all are determined by a free and pure sexual ebb and flow on the primary level. When love leads sexuality rather than animal lust, a high quality of life is the natural result and the rewards are great.

Sexual dynamics are designed into us as human beings. This dynamic is the unseen Director of History. Behind every historical figure having great impact on the movement and sway of people and events, is the scenario of sex. How goes sex, goes a man's life. How goes sex, goes this world. Peel back the layers of cell memory. Every great good and every great evil comes from the use or abuse of sexuality. The Creator uses man's sexuality to move in the drama of lineage and to fulfill His purposes in the Universe. The Books of Genesis, Exodus, and Leviticus in the Bible reveal a hair raising saga of sex, every day delight, sin, sorrow—and the need for a Savior. People can get lost if there is no proper protocol for the use of their sexual energies. Even with a proper protocol, man is left with the choice of observing or not, what is known to be right. In the stories of Abraham, Isaac, Jacob, Joseph and others in the Bible book of Genesis, sex is seen as a dynamic second only to the workings of the Holy Spirit, affecting the history of nations and the world. God opens and closes the spiritual eyes of men and women, works with their sexual propensities and chemistries, and thereby creates the materialization of His heart's desire. We, as human beings, do the same on a small scale. To the extent we understand sexuality and its power to uplift or degrade, we can move through life victorious, in the Zone of Holiness, or lose ground in the zone of profanity. Sex is not to be dealt with lightly.

What we know and what we understand, we teach others. Sexual truth and purity is to be taught by the example of attitude, behavior, the use of clothing, and carefully chosen words. Women have the primary responsibility for the direction of sexuality in this world.

***

In the area of sexual pressures, women and men can begin the journey away from profanity and into the Zone of Holiness by simply saying "No." In any situation, if you feel a pressure to be something you are not or do something against your nature or love impulse pattern, just say "naah!" What a true liberation this is. Women will often be well served to say "naah!" to protect their spiritual identity and their physical well-being. Men are well served to be just as protective of themselves. This is a vital area of spiritual discrimination and it is good.

Quietly underlying the sometimes over whelming effects of hormones, is a holy place of interplay between opposites. When a man draws a woman, he wants to give. When woman draws a man she wants to create something that has never been before. Something holy. Woman is the vestibule of Creation. God is the Creator. Man is God's eternal agent. Deep within man is the creative knowledge of how and why. Woman knows who and when. We attract others for all kinds of purposes. Electrical frequencies of sexuality resonate with other electrical frequencies that perfectly match the spiritual intentions of the people involved. Sexual attraction works for us automatically. Most of the time, the body is participating without noticeable involvement. All of life is about sexual attraction on some level. The dinner plate, at its best, is a play of opposites in taste, chemistry, and texture. Particular people are drawn together to fulfill the desires of God's Heart. We have less choice than we think in the mating game, and thankfully less responsibility. Our responsibility is to say a resounding "NAAH!" to activity *not authorized by the heart*. To know when God's high five is given in the area of sexuality is a vital area of discernment. Having "naah" ready until you are divinely certain is part of living in the Zone of Holiness.

Sex is a gift of delight to motivate creative work and bring children to our families. The creative power of opposites, in and beyond physical relationships, rejuvenates every part of being human. The way we express sexuality creates without words the story line of our lives.

Epilogue

The ripple effect and the power of momentum demand change. If you desire to live in the Zone of Holiness, any small choice made from your heart with this intention, creates a difference, moving you closer. If you can resist the temptation of the current moment to "self bless", the door to divine blessings begins to open. This is the point where our horizontal earth time meets vertical eternity—the golden point of "now."

In this world, particularly in highly developed cultures, "self blessing" is easy and a trap for the unaware. To take care of our selves is a personal responsibility. Nevertheless, over "blessing" self is profane and leads to missing the best. People try to bless themselves, sometimes desperately fearing it won't happen, but for their individual effort. The holy choice is to trust God to meet the need and work along with Him. As we do this He blesses us beyond what we imagine as our desires.

To "self bless" the energy of old cell memory is required—memory stored in our bodies that does not serve us. Even good cell memory can impede our evolvement. Waiting patiently for God to act in the areas of His prerogative, creates the energy frequency that correlates with accepting the gift of Christ. We then are in the *position* (energy frequency) for miracles to happen spontaneously. A mystery in spiritual science it is, yet Jesus cancelled all offending cell memory (sin) in every person, past, present and future with His work on the cross. It is finished, yet to individually claim His cleansing gift, we have to individually accept it with gratitude and seek to live in the Zone of Holiness. Every time we refuse to self bless and allow God to bless us instead, we move a little closer to Him and affirm our choice to thankfully accept the Savior.

There are seven affirmations, all beginning with the letter "R", that I enjoy and say at night before sleep or whenever I want to. I leave these with you in summation:

1. I Receive You, Jesus—Lord of All and my closest Friend— into the cells of my body. I thank you for what You did to save me.
2. I Release the energy from all offending cell memories and expel them from my body. I release the energy from all cell memory I do not need. I thank You, Jesus, for making this possible.
3. I Resist self blessing and wait instead for blessings from You.
4. I Recognize what I control and what You control.
5. I Realize who I am, with Holy choices.
6. I Remember my Rules and follow them.
7. I Reside forever in the Zone of Holiness—by choice, with love.

Spiritual and physical laws that materialize love, in the hands of holy choice makers, turn people who may perceive themselves as ordinary, into frontline heroes that will save our world, rescue our future and return joy, laughter, prosperity and peace to everyday life. As you make holy choices, you will begin to know yourself as never before. The Zone of Holiness will become more and more easily discerned. You will know with growing precision when to walk away from something or someone and when to engage. The ability to say a holy "no" is the beginning of self-love, which begins the ability to love another. In developing your awareness of the Holy Zone, you will learn when to say "naah" and when to say "YAAH!" Others will notice. God continues to reveal His plans to those who listen. The plans continue to evolve. The Holy Spirit continues to lead mankind away from profanity into the Zone of Holiness, our antidote to apocalypse.

Resources and Bibliography

KJV Super Giant Print Reference Bible. Nashville, TN: Broadman & Holman Publishers, 1996.

The Holy Bible, An American Translation. William F. Beck. New Haven, MO: Leader Publishing Company, 1976

Chopra, Deepak. *The Seven Spiritual Laws of Success.* San Rafael, CA: Amber-Allen Publishing and New World Library, 1994.

Gibran, Kahlil. *The Prophet.* New York: Alfred A. Knopf, 1927.

Hay, Louise. *You Can Heal Your Life. Carlsbad, CA: Hay House, 1984.*

King, Glenn. *An Introduction to TKM*: Self Help Book.* Carrollton, TX: King Institute, Inc. Publishers, 1996

King, Glenn. *Wonderfully Made.* Carrollton, TX: King Institute Ministries, Publishers, 2013.

L'Engle, Madeleine. *Walking on Water, Reflections on Faith and Art.* Wheaton, IL: Harold Shaw Publishers, 1980.

Lipton, Bruce. *The Biology of Belief.* Carlsbad, CA: Hay House, Inc., 2005.

Loyd, Alexander. *The Healing Code.* New York, NY: Grand Central Life & Style, Hachett Book Group, 2010.

Teeguarden, Iona Marsaa. *Acupressure Way of Health,* © 1978; originally published by Japan Publications, Inc., Tokyo, and since 2008 published by the Jin Shin Do° Foundation, www.jinshindo.org and distributed worldwide by JSDF and by Redwing Books, www.redwingbooks.com.

Teeguarden, Iona Marsaa. *A Complete Guide to Acupressure, Revised,* © 1996; originally published by Japan Publications, and now published by the Jin Shin Do˚ Foundation, www. jinshindo.org and distributed worldwide by JSDF and by Redwing Books, www.redwingbooks.com.

Teeguarden, Iona Marsaa. *The Joy of Feeling: Bodymind Acupressure˚,* © 1987; originally published by Japan Publications, Inc., Tokyo, and now published by the Jin Shin Do˚ Foundation, www.jinshindo.org and distributed worldwide by JSDF and by Redwing Books:

www.redwingbooks.com.

www.farmstay-ca.com. web site by Rod Burns and Geraldine Kenny.

www.moringasource.com. web store for moringa products.

www.singingzone.com. web site by Per Bristow.

www.wildernessfamilynaturals.com. web store for coconut products.

www.ingramcontent.com/pod-product-compliance
Lightning Source LLC
Chambersburg PA
CBHW021400090426
42742CB00009B/937